Collins New Advanced History Series

Reaction and Reform 1815-1841

J W Hu

Collins London and Glasgow

General Editors
K H Randell   J W Hunt

© J W Hunt 1972

Printed in Great Britain
Collins Clear Type Press
Set in Monotype Plantin

ISBN 0 00 327213 3

First published 1972

Fourth impression 1978

Cover illustration: Radio Times Hulton Picture Library

Contents

Editors' Foreword

The series of which this book is a part is designed to meet the needs of students in Sixth Forms and those taking courses in further and higher education. In assessing these needs two factors especially have been taken into account: the limits on the student's time which preclude the reading of all the important scholarly works, and the importance of providing stimulus to thought and imagination. Therefore the series, which has considerably more space available than even the larger single-volume textbooks on the period, presents the interpretations which have altered or increased our understanding of the age, as well as including sufficient detail to illustrate and enliven the subject. Most important of all, emphasis has been placed on discussion. Instead of outlining supposedly established facts, problems are posed as they were faced by the people of the time and as they confront the historian today in his task of interpretation. The student is thus enabled to approach the subject in an attitude of enquiry, and is encouraged to exercise his own mind on the arguments, never closed, of historiography. In so doing he will gain some knowledge of the methods of historians and of the kinds of evidence they use. He should also find enjoyment by the way.

The arrangement of the series, with several volumes covering particular aspects over a long period, and others with more strict chronological limits, has enabled each author to concentrate on an area of special interest, and should make for flexibility in use by the reader.

K.H.R.
J.W.H.

Full details of historical works referred to in the text will be found in the list of Further Reading on page 138. Only where the work is not included is a full reference given in the text.

Chapter I

The Old Order and the New Forces

1 **The condition of Britain in 1815** Britain escaped much of the upheaval that began with the French Revolution of 1789 and kept Europe in turmoil until the defeat of Napoleon at Waterloo in 1815, and might therefore have been expected to enjoy, in contrast to her turbulent neighbour across the Channel, an era of slow and gradual change. In politics the contrast was indeed of this kind, but in economic and social matters it was the reverse. In France economic development was slow, and social changes, despite the Revolution, anything but sudden. In Britain, on the other hand, something like an economic and social revolution took place by the middle of the century. There was a vast increase in production and a startling rise in population. A large and swelling urban proletariat came on the scene, and played its part in political developments. There was a permanent shift of power in government from the landowning aristocracy to the middle class. Yet these changes, while giving rise to much disturbance and alarm, did not issue in a violent revolution. How this was avoided, how the necessary reforms were in part achieved, in part neglected, between 1815 and 1841, are the themes to be considered in this book.

That Britain was nearer to revolution during this period than at any other time since the end of the seventeenth century is hardly open to doubt. There was a convergence of many factors causing dislocation and stress. Most obvious were the strains of war, which the government alleged to be solely responsible for the distress of the people. Economic warfare, waged by blockade and counter-blockade, had disrupted industry, causing bankruptcies and unemployment. Foreign markets were lost or gained with the changing fortunes of war, and many areas of Europe were slow to recover from its ravages. When peace came government expenditure was suddenly halved; to switch production to peacetime commodities was no quick or easy matter. Taxation had risen to unprecedented heights, and as the taxes were mainly indirect and levied on necessities, they bore with unfair harshness on the poor. The end of the war brought little relief, for the government's debt had soared to £861 million, and the annual burden of interest on this—over £30 million, paid mainly to the well-to-do—guaranteed a succession of unpopular budgets. Finally, a great number of men, probably not less than 200,000, were discharged from the armed forces in the space of a year or so to flood a far from buoyant labour market.

Even without the war, the scale and pace of economic change would have brought painful consequences.* The rapid increase of population, which had begun about the middle of the eighteenth century, continued during the war years. Its results are difficult to distinguish from those of other changes, and it may be, as the more optimistic writers have maintained, that it conveniently provided about the number of extra workers the expansion of industry required. On the other hand it may have prevented the less skilled workers from claiming the higher wages that a scarcity of labour would have called for. Most of the population still worked on the land, and while more workers had been needed to secure the fifty per cent increase in home production of food which saved Britain from starvation and defeat, and also to feed the growing population of the towns, the natural increase of numbers was so large that it exceeded the demand for labour. When the war was over the small leaseholders found themselves in difficulties; prices fell, the poor rate was a heavy burden, and they often lacked capital for the adoption of improved methods. With the fall in prices the labourers' wages were sharply reduced.

* For the economic history of this period *see* T. F. May, *The Economy 1815-1914* in this series

Some left the land altogether, others declined into pauperism in the villages, being obliged to apply for poor relief to supplement their wages even when they were in work.

The growing demand for labour in industry kept pace in general with the increase in population, which in Great Britain rose from 12.6 million in 1811 to 18.5 million in 1841 without any increase in the proportion of unemployment. The vast growth of the textile industries, the manufacture of the new machines, the expansion of mining (in 1800 Britain was producing nine-tenths of the world's output of coal), the building of new roads and canals —all these called for more workers. On the other hand a great many families which were dependent on domestic industry were unable to compete with the machines and suffered grievously, particularly the half-million hand-loom weavers, whose weekly wages sank from 14 shillings in 1800 to 7 shillings or less in 1834. If there was the alternative of work in a textile factory, there would be few jobs for men, and conditions for women and children were harsh in the extreme. The general standard of life in towns might be no worse than in the country, but those who worked in factories had to submit to the novel and unwelcome discipline of fixed hours of labour under the orders of an employer or overseer. The rapid growth of the new towns raised problems of housing, health and sanitation, and of public order, quite beyond the administrative resources then available. Worst of all perhaps was the new liability to fluctuations in trade. Not only the impact of events overseas, not only the consequences of bad guesses about costs, prices and markets, but also the apparently incurable tendency of the economy to produce a cycle of booms and slumps entailed recurrent crises with attendant waves of unemployment and near-starvation for masses of workpeople. Britain was afflicted by these to a major degree in 1825-6, 1836-7 and 1839-42, and on a smaller scale in 1816-17 and 1818-19.

The French Revolution had shown the close connection between economic disorder, with its hardship and hunger, and political disturbance. The connection was equally obvious and alarming in Britain during this period, and it seemed that the whole social order, built up through centuries of only gradual change, might be violently overturned, and with it the system of government happily established, as all right-thinking Britons believed, by the Glorious Revolution of 1688.

2 The social framework William Cobbett, whose *Weekly Political Register* was read by tens of thousands at this time, sang the praises of the old order, cursed the new machines and the businessmen who made money out of them, and believed that all would be well again if the countryman could recover his independence and if the squire would do his duty. James Mill, foremost of the 'Scotch feelosophers' whom Cobbett hated, demonstrated on the other hand the inevitable superiority of the middle class, repository of the social virtues and natural mentor in morality of the labouring masses. Cobbett's Golden Age was never to return. The economic and social forces of the nineteenth century were on the side of Mill.

In the eighteenth century most British institutions had been operated by and for the landowning class, at the head of which were the great aristocratic families whose mansions still adorn the countryside. Beneath these social peaks were many gentle slopes; society was finely graded throughout, so that every man knew precisely who were 'his betters'. But no rank, not even the highest, was closed; people were constantly rising into the grade above by success in making money, by marriage, or by the help of influential friends. The social ideal was possession of a landed estate, enabling its owner to enjoy leisure—which he might use well, practising artistic tastes or encouraging science or invention, or ill, in gambling and high living. By buying land the businessman could remove, or at least conceal, the stigma of trade, and his descendants could thereafter live in the only way proper to gentlemen—on the rents from an inherited estate. The rights of property were absolute and unquestioned; John Locke had said the purpose of 'civil society' was its preservation. Landowners owed no obligations in respect of their estates, as in the feudal period (though they consented in Parliament to pay taxes on them). They owned the game on their land and the minerals below it. They often had the right to select the clergy to fill the church livings. Sometimes they virtually appointed members to Parliament, or presented or sold seats to ambitious politicians. From the lesser landowners were drawn most of the magistrates, who enforced the law and dispensed relief to the poor.

The nineteenth century was to see the landowners displaced from their dominant position by the men who drew their wealth from industry and commerce. But these were slow to develop as a self-conscious class; the main ambition of the leading members of the middle class was to leave it. When middle-class people had votes they willingly used them to put land-owners into Parliament. They had not the grudge against the aristocracy that had so powerfully moved the French bourgeoisie. This was partly because the aristocracy was not closed to them, and partly because, as Professor Perkin has pointed out, the eighteenth-century system, though designed for landowners, admirably suited the rising entrepreneurs: it provided absolute security of property, the minimum of government intervention, and protection from foreign competition. There had also been a blurring of the horizontal division into classes by a vertical division into interests—the landed, manufacturing and com-mercial interests, with subdivisions such as the shipping, West Indian and East Indian interests. The pursuit of one's interests within the eighteenth-century political system usually involved getting the help of someone in a superior position, and indi-viduals were linked, not as members of a class but in a system of 'vertical friendships'. The adjective must detract somewhat from the usual meaning of the noun, but the links were strong and the system all-pervasive. At the foot of the ladder even the virtuous poor, with the help of a protector, might get special consideration in the distribution of relief.

This was in fact the eighteenth-century system of patronage. The main field of patronage, of course, was the filling of paid positions in government, from the highest to the lowest. What appears to the twentieth-century mind as corruption was accepted then as the normal and natural, indeed the only, way of staffing the government service. The resulting favouritism and in-efficiency were the less serious in that the functions of government were limited and relatively simple—except in time of war, when maladministration was apt to produce disaster, and often did.

If the formation of a class-conscious bourgeoisie had been hindered by opportunities of advancement and by the division into interests, there had been even less chance during the eighteenth century for the development of an urban proletariat or working class. This could only arise in large towns, and the early factories, dependent as they were on water-power, did not bring workers together in big enough numbers. At the end of the century the wars and the government's repressive legislation postponed further any attempt at mass organisation. But by 1815 the new towns were formidably large—Manchester held 137,000 people in 1811, Glasgow 112,000—large enough for the segregation of classes into different residential areas, and it was then that unmistakable signs appeared of the division of the nation into classes. The wars had aggravated the problems already arising from the growth of population and from economic change, and instead of the quiet pursuit of interests by the propertied men and the submission of the rest, both entered on a struggle for what they considered to be their rights. There was no mistaking the class appeal of Thomas Paine's *Rights of Man* (1791-2) or James Mill's essay *On Government* (1821). There were nation-wide movements of protest and campaigns to secure representation in Parliament. Moreover, distinctively working-class organisations were arising in many parts of the country for the first time: in addition to the steady growth of friendly societies there were the first attempts to build up national trade unions, and there were political organisations and newspapers for the working class.

3 The representative system The closely related themes of property and interest were at the centre of the British constitution as it functioned in the period from 1688 to 1832. Its great glory was, in the eyes of its defenders, that every interest had a voice in government, i.e. that every form of property was represented. People who had no property were, by definition, unfit to be represented directly—they had no 'stake in the country'; they were represented indirectly by men of property—the tenant by his landlord, the town craftsman by the borough M.P.s, and so on. What mattered was not actual but virtual representation: as long as there was a body of people in Parliament to speak for an interest, that interest was satisfactorily provided for; the method by which the members were elected was considered unimportant. From the point of view of men of property the interests represented in Parliament were in fact fairly comprehensive, including as they did the armed services, the law, agriculture, industry, commerce, shipping, banking, the colonies—even brewing. By extending the idea of virtual representation the dominance in Parliament of the landowning class could be justified, for many would have maintained that the landowners were by tradition and natural right the leaders of the nation. Nor would its spiritual welfare be neglected: in the Tory view at least one of the chief concerns of the ruling class was to maintain the privileged position of the Church of England, to which, since it was the national church established by law, all Englishmen should adhere.

The suggestion that a system of this kind spelt tyranny would have been instantly rebutted. It was held to represent, on the contrary, a perfect and delicate balance, in which neither the Crown, the monarchical element, nor the House of Lords, the aristocratic, nor the House of Commons, the popular, could assert undue power, each being checked by the other two. At the same time the executive branch of government was controlled by the legislature and regulated by the judiciary, so that every man's freedom was secure. This was the constitution described by the Duke of Wellington in a famous speech in 1830 as so perfect that if he were asked to draft a scheme of government for another country he could do no better than prescribe the British system in its entirety—except for a doubt that the inhabitants of any other country would be fit to work it.

Refusing to be dazzled by the Duke's description, we must examine the workings of government in Britain more closely. In doing so it is difficult not to judge by the standards of the twentieth century, when in Britain a high degree of honesty and competence in government is taken for granted. It is more reasonable, however, to ask whether the electoral system and the machinery of government in the early nineteenth century were not more appropriate to the early eighteenth, or to some earlier period when they were first evolved. For it was a process of evolution that had produced these institutions; they were the work of history—and as such, according to Edmund Burke, all the more to be revered.

The system of election to the House of Commons was not the same in the four countries it represented—England, Wales, Scotland and (since the Union of 1801) Ireland. In England moreover there were wide differences between the counties and the boroughs. Throughout the counties there was a single qualification for the franchise—the possession of freehold land which could be reckoned to bring in an annual income of forty shillings. Although in law the freeholder was dependent on no man, in fact voters were often subject to pressure. This could easily be applied when a man had freehold land which gave him a vote, but also held other land as a tenant. In many counties there were great landowners whom it was dangerous to offend. Where there was no landed magnate, the gentry would largely decide who should go into Parliament, because most county electors thought it their duty to vote the same way as their local squire. County elections were very expensive. Only to a small extent was this due to direct money bribes; hospitality and travelling expenses for the voters ran away with large sums. It is not surprising that county elections were not always contested—only nine were in 1807, only two in 1812. Often the great landed families in a county would agree to divide the seats, one going regularly to a Tory, the other to a Whig. Either would be likely to uphold the interests of landowner and farmer; indeed many of the county M.P.s put these concerns above party allegiance, and were recognised as men of independence, deaf to the blandishments of ministers and Opposition alike. The total of county members was small—80 for all England—compared with borough representatives, although the counties contained far more voters.

In the boroughs there was a bewildering variety of franchises, all of ancient origin, exercised altogether by about 100,000 persons. Halévy counts 53 boroughs where there was a really popular franchise, voting rights being held either by all or by most freeholders, or by all householders, or by those householders who paid local taxes ('scot and lot'), or even, at Preston in Lancashire, by all adult males. Then there were the 37 burgage boroughs, where the right to vote belonged to either the owner or the occupier of those properties held by burgage tenure from the lord of the manor. But in most English boroughs M.P.s were elected either by the members of the corporation (a small number of people usually, but not always, selected by co-optation from the wealthier citizens), or by the freemen; these were originally the members of the guilds or companies, but sometimes were honorary freemen, who might reside outside the borough, and might in some cases be numerous and poor. The Earl of Lonsdale, for example, procured the freedom of the borough of Carlisle for 14,000 coalminers in his employ, so that they could vote as he directed.

Under all these franchises there was opportunity for influence in some form to be brought to bear on the electors, and in the boroughs as in the counties it was often the influence of great landowners. Even in the boroughs with a wide franchise the number of voters might be very small, because if a borough had grown its boundaries would not have been enlarged, and if it had declined most of the people would have left. Thus in twenty-two of these 'popular' boroughs the number of voters was under 300; in nineteen more it was under 800; in only eight was it over 1000. In the burgage boroughs there might be very few properties which carried entitlement to a vote. All of these could be bought up by one man; if the vote was exercised by the owner he would cast it himself, and so nominate the two M.P.s; if by occupiers they, being the owner's tenants, would usually vote as he directed. If the voters themselves owned their premises, they could not be intimidated, but they could be bribed, and expected this at every election. In consequence of these conditions there were many boroughs where the vote was cast or determined by a single person, others where two or a very small number controlled the electors, others again where the voters were open to bribery. In the last two cases there could be contested elections, if the contestants could face the cost. Where, however, one person held all the properties with electoral rights he could put himself into Parliament (if he was not already there as a peer), set up one of his relatives or friends in a political career, or sell the constituency at each election to the highest bidder. Only if the family fortunes were very low would he sell the properties outright, for at each election while he held them he could expect a clutch of golden eggs. A limited but not unimportant number of boroughs were under government control, either because, as in a dockyard town, most of the voters were state employees, or because sufficient votes were bought with bribes out of Treasury funds. Finally, in some of the corporation boroughs and most of the freemen boroughs there would be a large number of voters. When the figure ran into thousands effective bribery would be impossible, though even then free beer and other inducements might be provided by the rival candidates, and the open declaration of votes on the hustings took place in an atmosphere far removed from judicial calm. An election was so expensive in the more open boroughs, and so pointless in those where a single patron had control, that many seats were not contested; in the elections of the period 1815 to 1832 about two-thirds of the members were returned unopposed.

In Wales, Scotland and Ireland the franchise systems were roughly similar to the English. In Scotland, however, they produced an absurdly small body of electors: 45 members were returned for the whole country by some 4000 voters, all of whom were controlled by great landowners. In Parliament the Scottish members regularly supported the ministry in office in return for a fixed allocation to Scots of places in government service. Wales returned 24 members, some counties being represented by only one member. Welsh voters were reckoned to be normally honest and independent. In Ireland a large number of forty-shilling freeholders could vote in the counties, but they could vote only for Protestants, and were controlled by Protestant landowners of English origin. One day, however, they were to be aroused to use their power in the Catholic cause.

Even in the middle of the eighteenth century the House of Commons thus elected had failed to represent the nation. Only half a million voters had any part in choosing it; of those only a fraction were declaring their own choice. Every interest but the landowners was under-represented. The electoral map had been drawn in the Middle Ages and in Tudor times and little altered since. A state of affairs that was already unsatisfactory in 1750 was blatantly anomalous by 1815, for large movements of population had created great cities that had no representation at all. The North of England had far too few seats compared with the South. A middle class growing in wealth and importance—and in consciousness of its importance—had only a weak voice in the country's affairs. A host of new and pressing problems were crying out for attention that a Parliament dominated by landowners was incompetent to give.

It would be a mistake, however, to think of the proceedings of the unreformed House of Commons as being entirely controlled by wealthy patrons or powerful families. While 300 M.P.s owed their seats to peers, and most of these were related to peers, it was not only the landowners who had a voice—more than fifty businessmen had made their way into the Commons by 1818. Even the client who was put in by a noble patron might be allowed to have a mind of his own, and the man who had bought himself a seat in Parliament, like Sir Francis Burdett when he represented Boroughbridge, would be quite independent. So there was always a handful of Radicals to champion popular causes and upset the complacency of the majority. Finally, the House was to give convincing proof, by reforming itself in 1832, that it was by no means hopelessly fettered to a social system that was passing and an electoral procedure that was obsolete.

4 King, Lords and Commons; Tories and Whigs There was substance behind the theory that power was divided among the three ancient institutions—Crown, Lords and Commons—in such a way that a balance was ensured. George III and his sons, despite their various personal shortcomings, by no means occupied the place of a mere figurehead. The King could, though certainly within narrow limits, choose a Prime Minister or dismiss him, and he expected to be consulted by the Prime Minister about the selection of the other ministers; at least he would claim to have one included whom he specially favoured or to have one excluded whom he specially disliked. He gave personal attention to many of the details of patronage. He could if he wished take advice from a small number of ministers or from persons who were not ministers at all. He was consulted on all matters of policy and, if he was sufficiently diligent, read all important government papers. His influence on the shaping of policy might therefore be considerable, even if it was only exerted negatively by obstruction; George IV gave his ministers a great deal of trouble in this way over Catholic emancipation. In the last resort the sovereign might veto a Bill that had passed through Parliament. This had not been done since 1709, and was never to happen again, but by threatening to use the veto George III had compelled Catholic emancipation to be dropped from the Act of Union between Great Britain and Ireland, and so forced the resignation of William Pitt in 1801.

The powers of the House of Lords were equal with those of the Commons, except in dealing with money Bills, and usually in this period a majority of Cabinet ministers were members of the upper House. Bills could be introduced in their lordships' House, and they could reject Bills passed by the Commons. In virtue of their hereditary and irremovable character, and by reason of their influence over so many members of the other House, the peers might have dominated public affairs but for one thing—the sovereign's power to create new peerages, which secured the monarchy against any attempt by a hundred or so peers to obstruct the government or dictate to the King who his ministers should be. This power had been exercised very freely during the reign of George III, though not for such dire reasons; 95 peers had been created at the behest of Pitt, and by the end of the reign the upper House had almost doubled in size. Some of the new peers were members already of peers' families, some were distinguished soldiers and sailors, some were leading lawyers, but some were heads of families newly come into wealth. In Halévy's words, 'The House of Lords was becoming more and more a house of noblemen, less and less a house of gentlemen.'

While thus enabled to keep a check on the House of Lords, the monarch could influence the House of Commons by using patronage to purchase support for ministers of his choice. This power, however, had been much reduced during the reign of George III, in whose hands it had appeared to his Whig opponents to be dangerous. The judicious award of pensions and appointment to posts in state service were not without effect on the attitude of some members of Parliament, but such members were not always regular in their attendance or to be relied on for their votes. And the flow of favours had so dried up that in the Parliament of 1820 only 78 members were personally enjoying patronage, and Prime Ministers were known to complain that too few offices remained at their disposal to reward meritorious service, and too few pensions to provide decently for superannuated ministers of the Crown. Lord Liverpool pointed out, moreover, that salaries had fallen so much in purchasing power that a government post was hardly suitable to offer to a gentleman. The days of safe and solid majorities stiffened by cohorts of placemen were over; the days of cohesive and well-disciplined parties were yet to come.

The King's ministers therefore had no impregnable position from which to defy the royal wishes, had they been determined to do so. But until 1830 the sovereign was fortunate in dealing with Tory ministers who on principle would maintain the powers of the Crown, and would shrink from forcing on him ministers or measures he objected to. As long as the belief was held that the King should choose his ministers, so long would sustained or 'formed' opposition bear the taint of disloyalty. For this reason the Tories who resigned from their offices in 1827 because they would not serve under Canning suffered pricks of conscience over what they felt to be disobedience to the sovereign. The Whigs had no such qualms, and this was one of the real differences between the parties. The Whigs maintained as a constitutional doctrine that ministers who did not possess the confidence of the House of Commons must resign. In the last analysis the Whig doctrine was borne out by the realities of parliamentary politics—

the monarch must accommodate himself to a Prime Minister who had the support of a majority in the Commons, because without that support government could not be carried on.

The actual power of a ministry therefore depended on the strength and certainty of the support it received in Parliament, where already the House of Commons was more important than the House of Lords when it came to the survival or collapse of a ministry, because it was held to represent the nation, and because of its power over money matters. Support would never be either certain or strong until the party system had developed to the point where ministers knew, at any rate in all but the most exceptional circumstances, that they had a solid majority of M.P.s behind them. Such a development was far from complete in 1815. The idea of party lacked respectability, because of the tradition that men of goodwill should seek the national interest, not engage themselves to a faction. The King's ministers liked to be described as such, not as 'Tories', and their supporters looked back nostalgically to the days when they were known as 'the friends of Mr. Pitt'. For the Whigs the name of Charles James Fox had equal magic, but had overtones that were more decidedly partisan.

After 1815, however, both Tory and Whig traditions showed new vigour, and were nourished for the next few years by the Pitt Clubs and Fox Clubs up and down the country, where the birthdays of the respective heroes were celebrated with banquets and resounding speeches. The situation in Parliament too, gave new life to old party traditions and attitudes. There was now some approach to a two-party system, despite the factions of which both sides were composed, and despite the considerable number of men in both Houses who had no firm party allegiance. The Whigs were proud of their name, which signified for them an unbroken tradition reaching back to 1688 and even to the Civil War. And the appellation 'Tory' 'crept in again', as someone said at the time. The Whigs did their best to fasten it on their opponents, while some of the government's supporters, especially the country gentlemen, actually liked to be so called. In fact the familiar terms 'Tory' and 'Whig' seemed to fit the situation, with two groups in Parliament opposed to each other on several of the main issues of the time. It would not be particularly difficult to analyse the behaviour of M.P.s of this period after the manner of the late Sir Lewis Namier, ascribing the behaviour of each to certain interests and family connections. The analysis would, however, leave unexplained the reasons why two groups of politicians, undifferentiated by any general economic or social characteristics, should have taken up contradictory attitudes on discontent and agitation in the country, parliamentary reform, foreign policy and (with qualifications) on the Catholic question.

Their disagreements could be described as a contest of principles, or—perhaps less generously—as attitudes rooted in the past. The Tories, traditionally the defenders of throne and altar, now regarded themselves as champions of law and order and opponents of dangerous innovations. They would resist any further reduction in the powers of the monarch, and would not persist in a policy of which he disapproved. In home affairs they were willing to stave off the dangers of subversion by suppressing the normal liberties if need be. Most of them, but not all, wished to uphold the privileges of Anglicans by refusing full political rights to Roman Catholics and Nonconformists. Abroad they were eager to co-operate with the monarchs of Europe against revolutionary menaces. The Whigs, again for historical reasons, found the role of opposition congenial, and, as usual with those in opposition, had more to say about political principles. They had always thought of themselves as friends of liberty, and believed they were in close touch with public opinion. (It was a fact that a larger proportion of their M.P.s than of the Tories sat for counties and 'open' boroughs, where opinion could be expressed at election times.) They were therefore less easily alarmed than the Tories about the danger from agitation, and less ready to meet it by suppressing the freedom of the Press and granting powers of arbitrary arrest. They were correspondingly more ready to seek remedies for current discontents—even, if pressed, to consider some change in the constitution. They had always embraced the cause of the Nonconformists, and now accepted that only with the grant of political rights to Catholics could the problems of Ireland be solved. They could voice their sympathy with struggles for liberty in Europe, unembarrassed, since they were not in power, by a too close concern for British interests.

In 1815 and for some years afterwards, the Tories, though lacking distinguished leaders, held together under Lord Liverpool. The big question which might divide them, Catholic emancipation, was by agreement left open; as the government did not intend to do anything about it disagreement could be indulged in with safety, and even members of the Cabinet were free to differ. There were, however, lesser but more urgent questions that might cause the government's followers to waver. Anything that touched the agricultural interest needed handling with care; even a show of concern for the welfare of commerce brought a complaint from Lord Redesdale that 'we are rapidly becoming a nation of shopkeepers'. Ministers were in a constant state of anxiety about their majority in the House of Commons and in fact were several times defeated on a division. So loose were party ties and so large the number of uncommitted members that in a House of 658 not more than a hundred members could be absolutely depended on. There was a middle group of members who voted different ways on different occasions, including the 'country gentry', who, though they would normally support the government, were disconcertingly proud of their independence. It was difficult too for ministers to keep in touch with parliamentary opinion. Party meetings were most rare; there were Whips but no party organisation to support them, either in Parliament or outside; informal gatherings in clubs and private houses—and gossip—had to be relied on instead.

The state of the Whigs was worse than that of the Tories. Lord Grey was acknowledged to have inherited the mantle of Fox, yet Grenville was recognised in 1815 as leader. Both announced retirement in 1817; Grey did not in fact retire, but remained inactive for long periods. Grenville and his family group broke away in 1817, and by 1821 they were to be found in the Tory camp, where they remained. With the head of the Whig party in the Lords it was important to have an effective leader in the Commons, yet from 1815 to 1821 the Whigs had none of any vigour, and from 1821 to 1830 they had none at all. Apart from

Catholic emancipation, which they all supported, the Whigs had various views on the questions of the day; they differed on parliamentary reform, on measures for the relief of distress and the repression of disorder, and on foreign affairs. Yet the Whigs did manage to take a line on these questions distinct from that of the government, so that the years 1815-20 saw a partial revival of the two-party system. It seemed most unlikely, however, that the Whigs would oust the Tories and take their place on the government benches. Even when the government was most unpopular the Opposition could only muster 150 votes. While a general election did not altogether fail to reflect changes in public opinion, it was almost impossible to overthrow a ministerial majority when only one-third of the seats were contested. Nor could the Whigs rest their hopes, as they had formerly done, on the heir to the throne: the Regent was by now as deep-dyed a Tory as his father. The only real chance for the Whigs would come from a split in the Tory ranks and a defection to the Whig side of the more liberally-minded supporters of the government, and of this there was no sign as yet. On the other hand, internal disagreement among the Whigs and the weakness of their leadership left them open to the taunt that they were not even an effective Opposition. While Lord Liverpool's government cheered its supporters only with the 1815 Corn Law and stern measures of repression, the Opposition failed to cheer its followers with anything.

5 Administration 'In England the central government did nothing to secure the public safety, provided no schools, made no roads, gave no relief to the poor. With the one exception of the postal service, the state performed no function of immediate benefit to the taxpayer. In the eyes of the public the state appeared only as the power that enlisted men and levied taxes.' (Halévy, *History of the English People*, Vol. I.) Apart, therefore, from the exciseman, always on the watch for untaxed goods and highly unpopular, it was local government that impinged on the lives of ordinary people. The smallest unit of government was the parish, which was controlled by the vestry, either an 'open' vestry, comprising all the people of the parish, or a 'closed' vestry, a kind of committee elected (when things were done properly) by the 'open' vestry. The parish officers, led by the constable, were also elected, usually for a year at a time, and were mostly unpaid, but if such professional people as a surveyor or a doctor were engaged, a small annual retaining fee would be paid. The chief concern of the parish was the care of the poor, for which a special rate was levied. The maintenance of roads and bridges and perhaps of a parish well were other responsibilities, but these would be few, for the vestry meeting could be relied on to keep down the rates, and therefore to be sparing with amenities, such as street-lighting, which would be a charge on them.

The parishes were supervised in the performance of their functions by the magistrates of the county, the Justices of the Peace. These, too, were unpaid, and were appointed on the recommendation of the Lord Lieutenant of the county, who was normally the greatest landowner. The J.P.s were always men of property; an increasing proportion of them at this time were Church of England clergy. A sense of duty, a desire to safeguard their interests, and a degree of self-importance all played a part in inducing them to undertake a heavy burden of work and responsibility. They dealt with all infringements of the law (remitting the most serious cases for trial at the assizes), sitting in quarter sessions, in full strength, to try cases with a jury, or dispensing summary justice when, two or three together, they held petty sessions. They were usually severe on offences against property, and especially on poaching. Enjoying the social eminence of substantial landowners, and also wielding power as employers of local labour, the J.P.s with their combined judicial and administrative functions were the undisputed lords of the countryside. The central government depended on them at every turn, but especially for the maintenance of public order. If this was threatened by any trouble more serious than could be handled by the constable and his assistants, a magistrate must be found. His best hope was to persuade or frighten the rioters into desisting. If this failed, he could call out the county yeomanry—a mounted volunteer militia, who trained for a few weeks each year and served without pay. They were not trained to deal with civil disturbance, but might quell trouble by means of a few arrests and at the cost of a few broken heads.

On the other hand a riot which started over dear bread or one of many other grievances might suddenly spread until a whole city was out of control. Then the only recourse was to call on the Army, as the government had done extensively to deal with the machine-breaking riots of 1811-12. In enduring sporadic outbreaks in both town and country the nation had to pay dearly for the lack of a professional police force, which most people thought would be a danger to English liberties. They were less conscious of the danger implicit in the special measures the government had to take when it convinced itself, as it did too easily in the generation after the French Revolution, that the country was riddled with subversive plots. These measures had first been worked out by the younger Pitt, and were applied in 1812, from February 1817 to January 1818, and from August 1819 to the spring of 1820. On each of these occasions the ministers reported to secret committees of both Houses certain information they had received from unspecified sources, i.e., from spies and informers. On the strength of these reports Parliament took special action, such as suspending Habeas Corpus for a period, which enabled suspects to be imprisoned without trial. When the period of emergency was ended an Act of Indemnity was passed to protect ministers from the consequences of any illegality they might have committed. In this way Parliament itself acted to suspend the liberties which were so often praised as the chief glory of the British constitution.

The Church of England was inevitably involved in the social and political order into which it had been built by law at the time of the Reformation. It served as a large field for patronage and political influence. Its bishops were appointed by the sovereign, and sat in the House of Lords. The lesser clergy were as a rule appointed to livings by lay patrons, usually landowners of the locality. Adam Smith had written in *The Wealth of Nations* (1776): 'The clergy naturally endeavour to recommend themselves to the sovereign, to the court, and to the nobility and gentry of the country, by whose influence they chiefly expect to obtain preferment ... Such a clergy, however, while they pay their court in this manner to the higher ranks of life, are very apt to neglect altogether their influence and authority with the lower.' Many of the clergy had large incomes and were able to enjoy life's pleasures while giving scant attention either to Christian doctrine or to their duties. The right of the Church to exact tithe was resented, as it had always been; it was levied on the occupier, not the owner, of land, and it was often paid in kind, which was much less convenient than cash. Pluralism was rife: one man might hold several benefices, sometimes far apart, so that many parishes had an absentee incumbent; there were 4000 of these even as late as 1838. The minister's duties were then performed, if at all, by a miserably paid curate who was no better off than a farm labourer. There were of course, some conscientious clergy, but they were too few to make much impact on the lives of the poor. In the new towns there were very few clergy of any kind; as the Hammonds put it, 'Churches were, like Members of Parliament, most numerous where least needed.' The Church was silent about the social evils and injustices of the time; indeed, the clerical J.P.s, as at Manchester, were active in repressing popular movements. Consequently the Church was bitterly attacked in Radical pamphlets. Hetherington, campaigning in *The Poor Man's Guardian* against the punishment of flogging in the Army, asked, 'What priest or swaddler [Methodist preacher] was ever known to denounce the atrocity from the pulpit?'

The Church of Scotland exhibited the same failings in a lesser degree. There had from the beginning been an element of democracy in its organisation, because there were no bishops, and wide powers were vested in presbyteries, which were local councils composed of ministers and chief elders of churches. But the ministers were usually appointed, as in England, by lay patrons, who would sometimes force their nominees on reluctant congregations. In Scotland too the message of the Church had been weakened by the latitudinarian ideas of the eighteenth century, and it was failing, as in England, to reach most of the new urban working class.

6 A time of crisis Great Britain in 1815 provides a classical example of a community in which economic forces are producing a new distribution of wealth and are changing the social framework, but in which the political structure of the bygone era remains unaltered. The British structure had been erected more than a century earlier on a basis of property, and the dominant power was therefore in the hands of landowners, who assumed their right to supremacy to be part of the natural order. Their status was hereditary; the House of Lords was their citadel and the House of Commons largely filled with their dependents, while the Church and the armed services helped to provide for their families. There had been no effective challenge to the landed interest; the other interests had many ties with it, and were able to flourish within the system though they had only a subordinate place in it. Moreover, Britain's world-wide commerce and her colonies were highly profitable spheres of activity for business men where no immediate clash with the landed interest was involved.

So Britain came through the eighteenth century without civil strife or serious disturbance. Even the changes of the Industrial Revolution, rapid as they were from the 1780s, seemed at first to be a welcome means of expansion rather than a source of strain. But changes of such magnitude were bound at least to create problems of adjustment, and these were intensified, and remedies for them postponed, by the wars, which added their own ordeals of hardship and hunger. No solution of these difficulties was to be expected from the leaders of the country in the period immediately following the wars. It is significant that they were more easily stirred by the horrors of the slave trade than by the sufferings of their own countrymen. The Tory leaders were moulded by the society of the eighteenth century, governed by its assumptions, ignorant of the unprecedented forces at work within the nation, unable to understand or feel for the common people. Even if they had had the will to solve the country's problems they had not the means; parish vestries and unpaid magistrates had not the makings of a public service; patronage and administrative efficiency were incompatible. In a Parliament of wealthy men politicians fought out battles that had little to do with the concerns of the people at large. There was small hope of reform, for such proposals as could get through the House of Commons were likely to be rejected by the House of Lords. All but the most imaginative politicians accepted distress as inevitable, while the less imaginative thought firm repression an adequate response to discontent. But the new forces could not be denied for long. The much expanded middle class was ready to insist on its claims, while the working class was being driven to revolt by sheer distress. In an increasingly industrial Britain neither would submit any longer to control by landowners; they would fight for a share of political power.

They would fight also for ideals. The French Revolution had made a powerful impact on British opinion. The principles of 1789 may have had largely English origins, but what the French had displayed in their Revolution was the determination to overthrow a government they condemned as autocratic and a social system they condemned as unjust. Revolution had been justified by an appeal to the natural and fundamental rights of man. An idea so simple and attractive found many adherents in England, though when war broke out the traditional hatred of the French proved stronger for most people than even such heady political doctrine. When the war was over these theories of popular rights came again to the surface, and were joined by many streams of thought, some religious, others flowing from the Enlightenment of the eighteenth century, which together produced a surge of reforming zeal more powerful than anything Britain had previously experienced. Indeed it proved too powerful for the government to resist, and after an initial spell of reaction, the period was to see a considerable instalment of reform.

Chapter II

The Reformers

1 The Radicals To achieve success in nineteenth-century Britain a movement for reform had to combine the removal of abuses, which in a changing society were becoming ever more intolerable, with the preservation of private property, which for persons of power and influence was an article of faith. There was ready to hand a system of ideas admirably suited to these requirements—the Utilitarian philosophy, of which the chief exponent in Britain was Jeremy Bentham (1748-1832). Because Bentham lived to see the passing of the Reform Bill, and because his influence on legislation was so great in the succeeding period, we tend to think of him as a man of the nineteenth century. But he is in fact an excellent representative of the eighteenth-century movement known as the Enlightenment. This was developed in part from the teachings of Locke; central to it was his description of human psychology, according to which we all come into the world with minds that are completely blank and empty except for a faculty of association. By means of this the impressions received through the five senses are linked together so that knowledge grows; there is no other kind of knowledge. This was a doctrine that threw doubt on many traditional beliefs, and also placed strong emphasis on environmental factors as determining the kind of people we become. Good teaching, good laws and good institutions make good people; but if teaching, laws and institutions are bad, vice and misery are the result. On this basis, writers began to question the value and rightness of hitherto accepted customs and authorities. They were much encouraged by the successful investigations of the physical scientists, represented in England by the towering figure of Newton, and saw themselves as applying scientific method to social and political problems with equal hope of accuracy and certainty, and therefore with a similar chance of convincing everyone who read their works. So, in France, England and Scotland particularly, a vigorous campaign of inquiry went forward. What was the use of the monarchy and the aristocracy? Did the laws make sense? Were the doctrines of the churches true?

To these questions Jeremy Bentham, like many philosophers of the eighteenth century, returned negative answers, most emphatically to the last, for he believed that Christianity had been the bane of civilisation, and that its moral and social ideals were pernicious. Because he had had a legal training and was of a practical turn of mind, he concentrated his attention on the English legal system, and ceaselessly asked of the laws and legal procedure, 'What use is it?' If asked in return, 'Useful for what?' he had a universal answer which he had learnt from Joseph Priestley, Unitarian minister and discoverer of oxygen (1733-1804)—'Useful in promoting the greatest happiness of the greatest number.' This was the principle of utility, and the Utilitarians, then known as Philosophic Radicals, believed that by its fearless application the lot of mankind could be vastly improved. The lawgiver had simply to calculate how many people would suffer, and how much, through the adoption of a particular measure, and how many would gain in happiness, and how much, then make his decision accordingly. To help him reckon how much, Bentham produced his 'felicific calculus', a sort of multiplication table of happiness. In it human pleasures (twelve in number) were listed in order of magnitude according to their duration, intensity, etc., with a corresponding list of pains (of which there were fourteen). The mass of people were expected to accept the results of this mathematical policy-making very readily, because men naturally seek pleasure and avoid pain, and have no other motives. Difficulty arises only when what gives pleasure to one man causes pain to another; it is for these situations that laws are devised and governments are needed, but their operation can and should be minimal.

It may seem strange that a doctrine so artificial, treating human beings as isolated units, and wilfully ignoring large areas of human conduct and experience, should not only have gained an important following but have inspired much of the remedial legislation of the nineteenth century. Yet in the circumstances of the time such a crude instrument could be useful. Britain had inherited from past centuries a vast tangle of laws and practices productive of waste, delay, inefficiency and injustice and beneficial only to the lawyers. To ask 'What use is it?' however far removed the question was from truly philosophical inquiry, often served an excellent purpose. In an age when new problems demanded attention and the welfare of millions came to depend on government decisions, it may have been not altogether misleading to consider how many people would benefit and how many would suffer from a particular line of action. The answers were sometimes unfair and sometimes cruel, as in the case of the new Poor Law, but less so as a rule than answers derived from tradition or prescriptive right, which generally prevailed until 1822. The Utilitarians, scorning abstract doctrines of natural rights, were thoroughly practical, and their ideas on most subjects, though dogmatic, were clear and consistent and not without a measure of truth. Nor did the Benthamites lack self-assurance or enthusiasm.

The main achievement of Bentham himself was the formulation of a set of principles as the basis for legal reform. To this task he brought a keen intelligence (he had proceeded from Westminster School to Oxford at the age of thirteen), and a great deal of learning. He was a bachelor and lived among books. He had little knowledge of the world, scorned history and tradition, and was suspicious of all government and all lawyers, whom he referred to as 'Judge & Co'. 'If rogues did but know all the pains that the law has taken for their benefit', he wrote, 'honest men would have nothing left to call their own.' Bentham's principles of legal reform were characteristically detailed and precise. He enumerated four kinds of sanction available to legislators, divided criminal offences into four classes, and elaborated thirteen rules for determining penalties. One of the chief was that the harm caused by the punishment must not be greater than that caused by the offence. On the other hand the suffering caused by the punishment must be marginally greater than the benefit expected from the crime. Armed with these principles, the Benthamites set to work on the country's legal and administrative heritage, and improved large sections of it. A great many of the reforms of the nineteenth century are clearly traceable to Bentham's influence, though it must of course be remembered that many of these remedies had been suggested to Bentham by the needs of the time, and were therefore apparent to other people as well.

Perhaps the most remarkable of Bentham's followers was Francis Place (1771-1854), who was at the centre of the Radical movement throughout its most important phase. He played a vital part in the repeal of the Combination Acts, in the campaign for parliamentary reform, and finally in the early days of the Chartist movement. Brought up in poverty, Place knew dire hardship in his early working days when employed as a leather breeches maker. Later he managed to set himself up in business as a tailor, and became fairly prosperous, employing a number of journeymen—and incurring the displeasure of some historians who have deplored his lapse into a bourgeois outlook. His tailor's shop was near Charing Cross; in the back room he set up a sort of working-men's library, which also became a Radical committee-room. M.P.s on their way to the House, particularly Burdett and Hume, would call in to discuss their plans with him. From here too he carried on a vast correspondence in his campaigns for a succession of Radical causes. Soon after 1815 he was taken under Bentham's wing, and was so successfully imbued with Utilitarian principles that he became an ally of the middle-class reformers.

By no means all Radicals, however, accepted the rigid doctrines of Utilitarianism, or could be described as in any sense 'philosophic'. Many were strongly individualistic, and were the more successful as propagandists for that reason. Two of them were before everything else journalists of genius. The first was Thomas Paine (1737-1809), who was unsuccessful as corset-maker and exciseman before he went to America and turned to political journalism, playing a large part in inspiring the resistance of the colonists to the British government. Back in England, he wrote *Rights of Man* (1791-2) as an indignant rejoinder to Burke's *Reflections on the French Revolution*. Many of his ideas would be acceptable today to all the main political parties, but when they were published they seemed radical indeed. They were coloured also by atheism, which helped to give them a bad reputation with people of orthodox views. Part II of his book, which contained his more detailed and startling proposals, sold 200,000 copies in a year. It continued to circulate in the post-war years, possibly to a total of a million copies, and its ideas must have reached a large proportion of the adult population. Paine, like many writers before him, harked back to an idealised Anglo-Saxon 'constitution' blamed inequality on the Normans, and proposed to rectify it by a redistribution of property a liberalised poor law old age pensions, universal free education, and disarmament—all to be brought about, of course, by a reformed parliament elected by universal suffrage. Paine's ideas became the stock-in-trade of the Hampden Clubs, and so were conveyed to an even wider public.

Paine died in America after a second and less happy exile, and his remains were reverently brought back to his native land by William Cobbett (1762-1835), whose influence was to rival that of Paine himself. Indeed it has been said that Cobbett was the only man who could have brought about a revolution in Britain in the post-war period. But it is difficult to see such an individualist as leader of a movement; E. P. Thompson, while acknowledging his genius, says with some reason, 'Cobbett's favourite subject was William Cobbett.' Thomas Carlyle, on the other hand, saw him as 'the pattern John Bull of the century', a description warranted by Cobbett's genuine love of England and its people, especially country people. This was demonstrated in *Rural Rides*, in which he described the journeys through the countryside which he began in 1821. Cobbett believed England had been a happy land before the growth of factories and large towns, and that it had been spoilt by various kinds of wrongdoers, whom he castigated in pungent prose, among them profiteering contractors, the royal dukes with their frequent scandals, and other Radical leaders, particularly Burdett, Hunt and Owen. As time went on Cobbett came to believe that the prevalent abuses were caused not merely by ill-intentioned individuals, but by 'the system', which he called 'the Thing', and at the centre of 'the system' were the men who manipulated the nation's money in their own interests. So bankers and stock-jobbers—even Whig politicians falling into second place—became the favourite target for his vituperation, and consequently for popular hatred. Cobbett scorned piece-meal reform, so convinced was he that 'the Thing' must be and would be swept clean away—perhaps by the force of his own fulminations. Cobbett's journal was *The Weekly Political Register*, which ran from 1802 to 1836. He evaded the stamp duty on news-papers by publishing a cheap edition at twopence in the form of a commentary, but when in 1819 the law was changed to bring it under the duty it was published clandestinely, and unstamped, and still sold 60,000 copies. In Lancashire, 'the mills turned out when the mail coach brought *The Political Register*.' Cobbett's paper stood up for the people at a time when there was little else to sustain their morale, and working-class Radicalism could hardly have survived through the difficult years of the early nineteenth century without the constant activity of the popular press which he pioneered.

While Cobbett's *Register* led the Radical campaign in print, its chief leaders on the platform were Henry Hunt (whose activities are described in Chapter III) and Major John Cartwright (1740-1824), who had been a naval officer and later a major in the Nottinghamshire militia. Place describes Cartwright as 'cheerful, agreeable, and full of curious anecdotes', but adds, 'He was, however, in political matters, exceedingly troublesome, and some-times exceedingly absurd.' Cartwright failed five times to gain election to Parliament, so waged his campaign for universal suffrage, annual parliaments and the ballot through his writings and by tirelessly addressing meetings throughout the country. He was for a time persuaded by Sir Francis Burdett, a Radical M.P. and for many years his ally, to accept a plan limiting the franchise to ratepayers, and in 1811 on this basis, they jointly founded the Hampden Club. This was to provide a body of leaders—originally every member had to prove his ownership of a landed estate and subscribe two pounds a year—and also to build up popular support for a new electoral system. To this end Cartwright, when in his seventies, went on long speaking tours in England and Scotland; Hampden Clubs sprang up in his tracks, their members now subscribing not two pounds a year but a penny a week. In this way, as well as through Cobbett's *Register*, the Radical movement reached out to the working-class people in the industrial towns, and universal suffrage was therefore restored to Cartwright's programme. Petitions were collected from his meetings and sent up to Parliament with impressive numbers of signatures.

In the House of Commons itself the number of Radicals was of course very small indeed. A Radical might arrive there as member for one of the few 'popular' boroughs like Westminster or Preston, or he might be wealthy enough to purchase a seat, in which case he could ignore the views of his constituents. In the post-war years the most active Radical M.P.s were Bennet, Burdett, Romilly and Hume. Henry Grey Bennet (1777-1836), son of a peer, concerned himself with the sufferings of child chimney-sweeps and conditions in prisons, and did more than anyone else in Parliament to expose the abuses of the spy system. In this he was supported by Sir Francis Burdett (1770-1844), who had married into the banking family of Coutts, and was very rich. He first entered the House as member for Boroughbridge, one of the Duke of Newcastle's pocket boroughs, but in 1807 he won an exciting election at Westminster, and so scored the first electoral success for the cause of parliamentary reform. In the House he was tireless in defence of free speech, and fought a fierce but hopeless battle against the suspension of Habeas Corpus in 1817. On one occasion, amidst great public excitement, he got himself arrested and imprisoned in the Tower for some weeks for defying the House of Commons on the question of publishing its proceedings.

Sir Samuel Romilly (1757-1818) specialised in penal reform, and his tireless advocacy succeeded in getting the death penalty removed from a small number of minor offences, though final success came only with Peel's measures of penal reform in the 1820s, which Romilly did not live to see. The speciality of Joseph Hume (1777-1855), a former army surgeon, was an annual dissection of the budget proposals. Every item of expenditure came under his expert scrutiny, and to him belongs much of the credit for the reduction of expenditure, and of taxes, in the Budgets of 1821 and 1822. Hume was also the most active spokesman in the Commons of the Utilitarian views which inspired most of the middle-class Radicals of this period.

2 The socialists A number of writers appeared at this time who did not believe in the sacredness of private property, and who must be described as pioneer socialists rather than Radicals, though the word 'socialism' was not used until 1827, in the discussions of the recently formed London Co-operative Society. Among these pioneers was Thomas Spence (1750-1814), who believed, like Cobbett, that there had been an earlier age of happiness when society had been based on the free tiller of the soil, but unlike Cobbett pinned his hopes on a complete revolution in the ownership of land. Hence he and others of his kind were derided by Cobbett as 'the Agriculturasses'. Spence engaged in a lawsuit against the corporation of Newcastle in order to preserve to the people of the town their rights over the town moor, and later published a book, *The Restorer of Society to its Natural State*, which earned him twelve months' imprisonment. He urged the people to resume their right to the land; everywhere this should be owned by the parish and leased to those who farmed it, the rent being the only form of tax. Spence had only a few followers, but they were tightly organised, were sworn to revolution, and led most of the big working-class demonstrations in London in the years 1816-20. The government considered—or pretended to consider—the Spenceans highly dangerous, and infiltrated their groups with spies, though many of them, like Spence himself according to Place's description, were 'unpractical in the ways of the world to an extent hardly imaginable'.

Far more influential than Spence was Robert Owen (1771-1858), described by Max Beer in his *History of British Socialism* as the first socialist not inspired by the past. Owen was indeed clearly inspired by the world he lived in, being convinced by the triumphs of the machine that an era of plenty was close at hand. This confidence stemmed partly from his own career. Starting as a draper's assistant, he set up a cotton factory in 1789 with £100 that he borrowed; twenty years later he was sole owner of the New Lanark cotton mills, having bought out his partners for £84,000 in cash. His success caused many people who would otherwise have ignored him to listen to his ideas. These were not always original, but Owen's character and achievements combined with the dislocation and distress of the post-war years to give them wide currency and great influence. He first became famous as a model employer, showing at New Lanark that profits could be made while providing good conditions and reasonable hours of work. No child under ten was employed. Schools were built for younger children as well as houses for employees, and not only houses, but roads, places of recreation and shops where goods were sold at cost price. People came from all over the world to admire the New Lanark community.

This did not satisfy Owen, however. Believing, with the Utilitarians, that the purpose of life was happiness, and seeing around him unemployment, poverty and wretchedness, he was filled with zeal to liberate mankind from its misery by a transformation of society. His scheme may have been utopian but it was not romantic. He was not harking back to an idealised past, but aiming, in G. D. H. Cole's words, at a 'social system based on the essentially co-operative character of modern large-scale processes of production'. Greed and competition, so far from making a better world, had been the cause of corruption and disorder. Owen was convinced, having absorbed the notions prevalent in the eighteenth century, that character was made by circumstances. People were wicked not because of original sin, as the churches taught—Owen completely rejected religion—but by the corrupt society in which they grew up. His new system would be a network of New Lanarks, co-operation within each unit and between them ensuring maximum production and general harmony. He wanted to set up 'Villages of Co-operation' to provide for the unemployed, and hoped that these would spread all over the world to replace the capitalist system. Confident of the efficacy of economic and social reform, Owen rejected political remedies. He was not interested in universal suffrage, and thought political agitation useless. He therefore deplored the activities of Cobbett and other Radicals, while Cobbett in return hated Owen's paternalism, and called his model villages 'Parallelograms for Paupers'. The fundamental difference was that Cobbett trusted the ordinary man, while Owen, compassionate as he was, did not—at any rate until men had been reformed by living in an Owenite community. That Owen received a respectful hearing from Lord Sidmouth and even from the Duke of York did nothing to endear him to the Radicals, and the failure of several Owenite settlements, especially 'New Harmony' in Indiana, U.S.A., caused them no grief.

The distress of 1816, when there was widespread unemployment, put Owen on to a new train of thought. He saw thousands of people being barely kept alive on a pittance when, he argued, they could be profitably employed in producing the goods they lacked. By 1818 he had broken away from the Utilitarians, who accepted the teaching of the economists, particularly Malthus's dictum that population must always outrun the means of subsistence. On the contrary, declared Owen, man's productive capacity had increased much faster than the population; he estimated that output was fifteen times greater after than before the wars. The whole trouble was that the workmen were paid in wages much less than the value of what they produced, the surplus being taken by the employers, who exported it to foreign markets while they could, and turned off their workers when they could not. In expounding this theory Owen was the first person to explain unemployment as being due to under-consumption. The remedy, which in some places had a temporary success in the 1830s, was to pay workpeople in 'labour notes' instead of money; these represented the full value of their work, and enabled them to purchase an equivalent quantity of goods produced by somebody else. Abundance could then create happiness instead of misery. Owen's teaching gained a large following in the troubled years from 1815 to 1832, and he left almost all later socialists in his debt by giving substance to the labour theory of value and by focusing the antithesis of capitalism and socialism more sharply than ever before.

3 The Methodists and the Evangelicals

That Paine, Place, Owen and many other leaders of reform movements in this period were militant unbelievers obviously did not prevent their gaining a large following among working-class people. It certainly increased the fear and hatred felt for them by the government and the men of property, for whereas in the eighteenth century scepticism was fashionable and the Church of England itself so broad in its beliefs as almost to abandon orthodox Christianity, after the French Revolution religion was seen as an indispensable support to law and order and there was a general return of the ruling class to the faith. But it was not only dread of revolution, or of divine displeasure, that had converted the upper classes. The Methodists and Evangelicals had preached righteousness to such good effect that the nation seemed to regard itself in a new light, to think of Britain 'as being at once the home of liberty and virtue'.

The war period saw a remarkable growth of the Nonconformist sects—not so much of the older denominations, the Presbyterians, Congregationalists and Baptists, who had lost their missionary zeal, but of Methodism, which despite the intentions of John Wesley, its founder, had become a new sect, and the most thoroughly organised and effective of the Nonconformist bodies. It is probable that by 1815 the Anglicans who went regularly to church were in England equalled in number (while in Wales they were exceeded) by the Nonconformists—and the majority of these were Methodists.

The vigour of the Methodists was seen not only in the rapid increase of their chapels and their congregations. They had an influence both on the other sects, which copied their organisation, and on the Church of England, within which a similar movement appeared. It began with small groups of laymen of Low Church inclinations, who came to be known as Evangelicals. These groups were originally inspired by Wesley; like him, they wanted to endow the Church with a new religious fervour, but they remained within it. They were passionately eager to save souls, and they urged upon their fellows a complete emotional commitment to God and an irreproachable strictness of behaviour in daily life. At the same time they were ready to combat evil and to alleviate suffering wherever they found it, and so became prominent in movements of reform. One group, composed of laymen of some wealth and position, was formed at Clapham, near London, and came to be known as the Clapham Sect. Their leader was William Wilberforce (1759-1833); many of them, like him, were Members of Parliament, and because they stressed their moral standpoint in politics they were called, in derision, 'the party of the Saints'. They played an important part in the nation's affairs, however, partly because in furtherance of their aims they allied themselves with members of other sects, or even with men of no religion at all.

The great triumph of the Evangelicals and their friends had been the abolition of the slave trade by Act of Parliament in 1807, and their next aim, of course, was to forbid the practice of slavery in the British colonies. Meanwhile Cobbett and others were not slow to allege that in their anguished concern for black slaves overseas the abolitionists failed to notice the sufferings of the factory children at home, who often toiled in similar conditions. The charge was not altogether true. Evangelicals helped to secure the passage of the early Acts, largely ineffective though they were, to improve the lot of children employed as chimney sweeps and in factories, and later it was a persistent campaign inspired by Evangelicalism and led by Lord Shaftesbury that produced more satisfactory measures. Wilberforce supported the efforts of Romilly in the Commons to reduce the infliction of the death penalty, and the Evangelicals helped to turn public opinion against duelling and cruel sports. They showed even greater enthusiasm, no doubt, for measures to enforce the strict observance of the Sabbath, but altogether it may be claimed that in sensitivity to social wrongs and in the persistence of their endeavours to remove them the Evangelicals had few equals.

Chapter III

Repression

1 **The government: personalities and policy** Though it enjoyed the triumph of final victory over Napoleon in 1815, the government which, with little change of personnel, remained in office from 1812 to 1822 shed its clouds of glory only too soon. Most of its members were undistinguished, and they were led by a man of colourless personality who lacked the more obvious qualifications for the post of Prime Minister. The ministry's domestic policy was largely negative, and it was without question the most repressive government Britain had known since the seventeenth century.

The members of this government were not all aristocrats; they had rather the character of thoroughly professional politicians. That Robert Jenkinson, second Earl of Liverpool (1770-1828), should have been at the head of affairs continuously for fifteen years (1812-27) must seem something of a mystery. Disraeli was to describe him, in *Coningsby*, as 'an arch-mediocrity', and if this was too harsh, he was certainly dull and totally uninspiring. Though dutiful, he hardly had a zest for business. He was reported to have said himself that he 'viewed every morning's letters with such distaste that he could hardly bring himself to open them'. However, his background and experience gave him some qualifications for high office. His family had belonged to the country gentry, his father being raised to the peerage for political services. On taking up politics he gained much experience in a number of important ministerial positions before he became

Prime Minister in 1812 on the assassination of Spencer Perceval. Liverpool's main interest was in the economic progress of the country; he welcomed the growth of industry and commerce, but being a believer in laissez-faire, did not propose to assist it by government action. His qualities of character made him generally respected: he was honest and straightforward, he had business capacity and cool judgment, tact and ability to manage men. He was a great conciliator; he could get on with his colleagues, however diverse, and hold their loyalty however antagonistic they were to one another. It has been suggested also that he stayed so long in office because he had no distinct band of followers; if this meant that he lacked support, it also saved him from continual factional strife.

Henry Addington, Viscount Sidmouth (1757-1844), was the son of a well-known London physician. He was for many years Speaker of the House of Commons, and after Pitt's resignation was Prime Minister from 1801 to 1804. From 1812 to 1822 he was Home Secretary, and was therefore primarily responsible for the measures of repression during that period, though he has been described as 'kindly by nature'. His last speech in the House of Lords was to be against Catholic emancipation, and his last vote against parliamentary reform—a consistent record. John Scott, Earl of Eldon (1751-1838), having already been appointed Solicitor General in 1788 and then Attorney-General, was Lord Chancellor from 1801 to 1806 and from 1807 to 1827, holding the position longer than anyone else has ever done. He was the son of a Newcastle coal merchant, and was destined for the Church, but an elopement necessitated the choice of another career; he continued, however, to be fascinated by theology. He became the finest lawyer of his day, and was quite sincere in his belief that as the government of Britain was perfect, people who sought to change it deserved no mercy. He accordingly found a congenial task in helping to draft the repressive legislation of 1817-19, and resisted every attempt to moderate the rigour of the penal system.

Robert Stewart, Viscount Castlereagh (1769-1822), was the eldest son of an aristocratic family, and as Foreign Secretary found no difficulty in mixing with the sovereigns and statesmen of

Europe. He had held a responsible post in the government of Ireland before he was thirty, and attained Cabinet rank by 1802. In 1809 he fought his famous duel with Canning on finding that the latter was plotting his removal from office, an episode that led to the temporary retirement of both. From 1812 almost till his death by his own hand in 1822 he carried the double burden of the Foreign Office and the leadership of the government in the House of Commons. His duties as spokesman for the government there, while most of his ministerial colleagues sat in the Lords, gave him greater weight in the Cabinet. For the same reason he was closely identified in the public mind with the measures of repression that he expounded and justified in the lower House, though of course his attention was given mainly to foreign affairs.* He hardly deserved the special odium attaching to his name; it was his colleagues in the Cabinet who pressed for harsh measures, and on Irish and economic affairs he took a comparatively liberal line. But as a speaker he was awkward and his disdainful air in face of criticism, whether due to haughtiness or shyness, was more calculated to make enemies than friends.

The Duke of Wellington (1769-1852) joined the ministry in 1818 when the military occupation of France came to an end, and followed his military career with an even longer one in politics. He brought to it the mind and temper of a soldier who was also a thoroughgoing Tory, but he was to show in more than one crisis a sound sense of realities, while his great reputation gave him unusual influence with ministerial colleagues and with the sovereign.

As soon as the war was over, the government was faced with economic problems (described in Chapter I) daunting in their scale and novelty. Far from tackling them with bold measures, the government remained for the most part inactive, partly because it held to a belief in the doctrine of laissez-faire and the uselessness of state interference, partly because it attributed the troubles to the war and expected time to remove them, and partly because it was without the expert advice and administrative competence that would have been required for effective action. Yet two measures were promptly taken which bore every appearance of class

*See D. R. Ward, *Foreign Affairs 1815-1865* in this series

legislation of the most selfish and callous description—the new Corn Law of 1815 and the repeal of the property or income tax imposed in 1798.

The Tories, and many Whigs, could commit themselves to the protection of home-grown corn, in flat defiance of laissez-faire principles, on the almost unconscious assumption that the landed interest was of unique importance and must receive special consideration. The object of the law of 1815 was to prevent a fall in the price of corn from its wartime levels to a figure which would endanger the profits of the farmers and the rents of their landlords—the rents which were the main economic foundation of an aristocratic social order. 'If farmers defaulted on their rents, three-quarters of the House of Commons felt the pinch.' Profits and rents were to be secured by a total ban on the import of cereals except when prices in Britain reached certain levels, in the case of wheat when the domestic price rose above 80s a quarter, when it could be imported free of duty. (A quarter, 24 bushels, was about the amount an adult, with bread as his staple food, would consume in a year.) The price had reached 80s in 1808; in 1812 it had risen to 126s, but in 1813 it was down to 73s, and early in 1816, thanks to a good harvest in the previous year, it was only 48s. But later in 1816, after a poor harvest, the price was up to 103s. At this figure a large proportion of the wage-earners, including the agricultural labourers, would be unable to buy bread, and would fall back on oatmeal in Scotland and the north of England, on potatoes in the south. At 80s bread would still be beyond the means of the poorer wage-earners with size-able families. To the Radicals the Corn Law was the supreme demonstration of the corrupt character of the unreformed Parliament and the wickedness of the country's rulers.

The Corn Law was not, however, a gratuitous gift to a prospering agricultural industry. The government's fears were borne out by an agricultural depression which lasted from 1816 to 1825. This was partly a reaction from the feverish expansion of the war years, which had been made possible, in spite of its great cost, by inflated prices. Marginal land had been brought under cultivation, giving a poor yield for extra investment—often of borrowed money. When the war was over prices slumped, and the farmers, also harassed by exceptionally heavy poor rates, could not pay interest on their debts, nor repay the capital they had borrowed. Nor could landlords any longer extract the increased rents. Agriculture was therefore genuinely in difficulties.

Liverpool said, apparently sincerely, that his object was to assist the consumer. This would be achieved by keeping marginal land in production, so ensuring a plentiful supply. He believed, however, that the duty would establish 80s as the maximum, not the minimum price. He went far in professing his good intentions: 'Were the measure one which stood upon the narrow ground of affording relief to a particular class I would not support it . . . You cannot relieve one class of people without injuring some other class more or less'—an unexceptionable laissez-faire sentiment. The Bill, though presented in the Commons with some reluctance by Robinson, Vice-President of the Board of Trade, met with little opposition. The government relied mainly on the argument that in years of difficulty it was impossible, and in time of war it was dangerous, to rely on foreign supplies, and forecast reduced prices as a result of the stimulus to production. If the forecast had been believed, support would have been less enthusiastic. The Leader of the Opposition agreed with the measure, and the case for free trade went by default. Outside Parliament the reaction was different: Robinson's house was attacked by a mob, and two of the crowd were shot; Robinson was reduced to tears in the House of Commons—a display of feeling to which he was distressingly liable.

The forecasts of lower prices were borne out to some extent—apart from 1816-17 the general trend was downwards—but this was due rather to good harvests than to any effect of the Act of 1815. Nor did it succeed in steadying prices. On the contrary, it produced sudden fluctuations when the dealers held back supplies to force prices up to the 80s mark, and then imported foreign corn until the price sank back again. It was thus the dealers who gained most from the restriction, while the price could still fall low enough to ruin the farmers or rise high enough to starve the consumer. The working of the Act was so unsatisfactory that it lasted only till 1822, when it was modified by the institution of a duty on a sliding scale.

In general the Corn Law of 1815 may have done less harm to the common people than the abolition of the income tax, from which incomes under £50 had been exempt, and which had to be replaced by further taxation of articles of general consumption. The promise made when the tax was imposed to remove it at the end of the war was not unconditional, and the government wished to continue it, but was overborne in 1816 by a flood of petitions, an eloquent attack launched by Henry Brougham, and a majority of the House of Commons. As the tax had yielded £15m. about a fifth of the revenue, in 1815, and as at the same time the wartime increase in the malt tax was removed, to the great satisfaction of the country members, the total loss of revenue was serious. The rebellious members were partly motivated by the failure of the Corn Law to improve prices; they declaimed about the impossibility of paying wartime taxes out of peace-time profits. But the manufacturers and the businessmen of the City of London were as loud in their complaints as the landed gentry. Those who had most reason to complain, however, were the poor people of both town and country, who were now bearing a bigger share of a burden largely due to the cost of the armed forces (still over a hundred thousand men) and the interest paid to holders of government stocks. It was not long before their discontent burst forth—in disorders which required the use of the armed forces for their repression.

2 **An unhappy country, 1816-1819**　The first outbreak of disorder occurred in the eastern counties in protest against falling wages and rising food prices. There is no doubt about the worsening of the labourers' conditions, although it has not been determined whether this was in part due to enclosures, as well as to more temporary factors. Whatever the causes, their position was desperate, and they resorted to arson, the smashing of threshing machines and other attacks on property to press their demands for relief. Soon there were also demonstrations and strikes, often attended by violence, in a number of industrial districts from

South Wales to Newcastle. Many rioters were brought to trial, and several were executed. In London the demonstrations were more massive and organised with more care, by men who aimed to make the capital the centre of a nation-wide agitation. But in fact the main impetus continued to come from the provinces. London was so large, and its crafts and patterns of employment so various, that it was difficult to secure any cohesion among its workpeople apart from the occasional unanimity of a mob. Even this was not always achieved. In 1816 the Spenceans planned a mass meeting in Spa Fields to agitate for Spence's programme of land reform, and invited Henry Hunt, the most prominent Radical orator, to address it. He, however, had no belief in land reform, and wanted to use the platform to advance the normal Radical plans for lower taxes and the reform of Parliament. After some confusion two meetings were held on the same December day. Fired by the violent propaganda of the Spencean meeting, a mob marched through the London streets, looting a few shops and letting off a few firearms. The tricolour had been raised, and revolutionary cries had been uttered.

Meanwhile the Radical leaders in the Borough of Westminster, Burdett and Place, with Bentham's close disciple James Mill, were organising a more moderate kind of demonstration. They planned a meeting in London to which the Hampden Clubs throughout the country should send delegates, two from each, bearing petitions for the reform of Parliament. After a meeting of all the delegates had passed the appropriate resolutions, a comprehensive petition would be presented to the House of Commons. Cobbett, Cartwright and Hunt were brought in to address the meeting, which was held in January 1817 at the Crown and Anchor Tavern in the Strand. The proceedings at that well-known centre of Radicalism were orderly but disappointing, especially to working men like Samuel Bamford who had come up from the provinces expecting a great occasion and prepared to admire the leaders of whom they had heard so much. Burdett absented himself from the meeting, yet Cartwright and even Cobbett deferred to his views by limiting their proposal to household suffrage, which meant restricting the vote to ratepayers. Hunt rejected this, and finally a vote demanding universal suffrage was carried, and the petition delivered at Westminster. The delegates dispersed, confused by the dissension among their leaders. On returning to their homes they were soon to find themselves the objects of a determined campaign of repression.

Already alarmed by the Spa Fields meeting, the government was ready to see the activities of the Hampden Clubs as a plan for nation-wide revolution, a view to which the alarmist reports from magistrates in the provinces gave the required colour. The developments of 1817 were to give it also some substance: the general disillusionment with the Crown and Anchor meeting and the government's resort to repression produced an atmosphere in which conspiracy took the place of open propaganda, and in which, therefore, *agents provocateurs* could ply their trade with success. The general support of the propertied classes, fearful of a proletarian rising, appeared to convince the Cabinet for the moment that no special measures were necessary, though Sidmouth pressed for them, and carried on a busy correspondence from the Home Office with magistrates all over the country, warning them to be in readiness and to suppress disorder with the utmost severity. When, however, the Prince Regent on his return to the Palace from the opening of Parliament in January 1817 had the window of his coach broken by a stone or a bullet, the government took stern measures. Most alarming evidence, produced by Sidmouth's spies, was reported to Parliament. An Act to suspend Habeas Corpus, so that people could be consigned to prison on suspicion only and without trial, was introduced into the Lords; it was put through both Houses within a week, with the support of some Whig as well as the Tory votes, and it remained in force for eleven months. The Seditious Meetings Act, also passed in 1817, imposed most stringent conditions on the holding of public meetings, and this was not a temporary measure. Equally important in its consequences was an instruction of Sidmouth to the magistrates, of dubious legality, that they had the right to arrest anyone engaged in the public sale of blasphemous or seditious literature. What followed is described by Halévy thus: 'The counter-revolutionary terror which had prevailed since

December [1816] increased in severity, and was now under the open patronage of Lord Sidmouth and his colleagues. No more public meetings were held, and the Hampden Clubs disappeared. The City magistrates refused to sanction a debating society, on the ground that the Government desired to put a stop to all political discussion . . . A magistrate refused his sanction to a mineralogical society on the pretext that mineralogy led to atheism.' The government could obviously rely on the local guardians of law and order to make full use of the gag it had provided. Cobbett was forced to flee to America, and Radical as well as revolutionary groups broke up in confusion. Just as reform movements were getting under way the middle class was frightened off them and the defenders of order and property on the one hand confronted the mass of the people on the other.

Unrest was intensified in 1817, when the sufferings of the industrial population were increased by the high cost of living, low wages and unemployment. In Manchester, where many of the hand-loom weavers were starving, a march to London was organised in the spring of 1817 in order to present petitions for reform to the Prince Regent. Each man was to carry a blanket and such provisions as he could afford, so it was called the March of the Blanketeers. It began with a mass meeting in St. Peter's Fields. The magistrates had the troops descend on this and arrest the leaders, and bands which had started on their orderly march to London were broken up. Several men were put in prison, but released after some time without being charged. Various alarming rumours were circulated about the marchers' intentions; the worst that could be truthfully said about them was that they were agitating for higher wages, lower prices and the reform of Parliament.

The Pentrich Rising was a different matter. This, though it turned out a miserable fiasco, was a conspiracy to bring about an armed rising. The plan was to stir up the people of Derbyshire, to seize Nottingham, and if successful so far, to march on London. The leader was Jeremiah Brandreth, an unemployed knitter and a Methodist. His followers seemed, not surprisingly, to be mainly interested in laying hands on good supplies of food. The conspirators were seized with arms in their hands and without difficulty because Oliver, the government spy, had gained their confidence and kept it just long enough to escape their vengeance. Nineteen of them were sentenced to death, of whom four were executed.

The Government's gagging measures had driven all reform movements underground. Instead of the open meetings of the Hampden Clubs there were secret societies, necessarily involved in conspiracy and easily infiltrated by spies, who gave them false information of proceedings elsewhere and urged them on to more dangerous courses. There is little doubt that this was the Government's chosen means of bringing revolutionary leaders into the open, so as to convince moderate opinion of the danger of revolution and justify the measures of repression, and even perhaps to divert the public mind from taxes and other causes of the government's unpopularity. But the method was far from successful. A London jury acquitted Dr. Watson, a Spencean leader, because the major evidence of his revolutionary intentions was that of a government spy. A week after the Pentrich Rising *The Leeds Mercury* revealed the full story of Oliver's part in it, to the great discredit of the government, which thereafter was somewhat more circumspect in its use of spies.

The Pentrich Rising had been a mad and ill-planned enterprise. Were more systematic preparations for an armed rising totally fabricated or inspired by spies? The Hammonds, in *The Skilled Labourer*, and Cole and Postgate, in *The Common People*, hold that they were. But E. P. Thompson speaks of 'overwhelming evidence' that some kind of 'physical force' conspiracy was afoot in 1817. Holdsworth is less positive, but considers that there is some evidence of the kind. There were certainly contacts between the 'Jacobin' party in London and extremists in the provinces, where small caches of arms were prepared and 'news' from London or Birmingham was always being awaited as the signal for a rising. Samuel Bamford, the weaver from Middleton, Lancashire, may have truthfully described his activities as non-violent in his attractive *Passages in the Life of a Radical* (when he was interrogated by Lord Sidmouth each found the other surprisingly gentlemanly), but some of the associates he describes were desperate men, and needed little incitement to illegality by *agents provocateurs*.

In 1817 there were an excellent harvest and the beginnings of a trade revival, so the next year brought some easing of hardship in most areas. There were frequent strikes in the industrial north, however, in an attempt to return to better wages, and efforts to form trade unions were harshly repressed by the magistrates. With 1819 came another trade depression; wage reductions and unemployment brought many workers to the point of despair. Their attempts to get wages improved or the Corn Law abolished had met with no success; a basic reform of Parliament seemed to be the only hope. Petitions to the House of Commons, backed by monster meetings, were still the usual plan of action, but the Radicals of Birmingham conceived a new idea: since the majority of the people were denied representation in Parliament, they should elect their own representatives and send them to London to assemble and to pass the necessary measures for the country's welfare. At a large but quite orderly meeting in July Sir Charles Wolseley, a democratic member of a famous family, was chosen by a show of hands. Similar action was part of the original programme for the meeting held in St. Peter's Fields, Manchester in August.

3 Peterloo Manchester had already been the scene of a good deal of unrest; the renewed economic depression, which particularly affected the hand-loom weavers, was bound to cause more. The programme of the local Radicals, men of no particular social standing or experience of affairs, was simple. They wanted an end of distress, and they believed in political rights for all. Their desires and their beliefs pointed in the same direction—the representation of the people in Parliament. They had picked up their ideas mainly from the Radical press, from which they learnt also to attack the Combination Laws and the Corn Law, and to declaim against the National Debt and the banks. Many employers and business men in Manchester agreed with much of the Radical programme; they had ample reason to be dissatisfied with the government's failure to manage the economy and with the chaotic administration of local affairs, and they certainly wanted Manchester to be represented in Parliament. But they did not approve of the methods of the working-class Radicals. In fact the programme of big meetings, the drilling, the wild talk, and the personalities of the Radical leaders, especially Henry Hunt, had filled the Manchester bourgeois with fear, almost to the point of panic, of a mass revolt and an outright attack on property. They believed they must act to prevent an insurrection, which, since the Radical movement was nation-wide, might easily flare up into a revolution, but the government was loth to employ armed force until there was clear evidence of sedition. Dr. D. Read shows, in *Peterloo*, that Lord Sidmouth had privately rebuked the magistrates for arresting so many of the Blanketeers' leaders on a charge of high treason when there was no evidence to justify such a charge. And while he had urged on the magistrates the utmost watchfulness, Sidmouth had also urged restraint: troops should not be used unless there was a breach of the peace.

The meeting which ended in the Peterloo massacre was deliberately located in Manchester as the most active centre of Radical agitation, and was intended to be the greatest manifestation of the popular will that Britain had ever seen. Contingents were expected from the whole of the area within marching distance. Drilling had taken place, it was stated, so that such a huge crowd could be handled in an orderly way. No weapons were to be carried. All the best-known Radical leaders were to be on the platform, and the main speech would be made by 'Orator' Hunt. Of Wiltshire yeoman stock, he was tall, and had a fine carriage and a stentorian voice. While he was by most accounts very vain and full of his own importance, he had practised the art of demagogic oratory to perfection, and kept to a consistent line, attacking taxation and corruption and demanding the reform of Parliament.

In order to avoid the illegality of the Birmingham meeting, the plan to elect a representative of the people was dropped. The meeting would not be illegal if it was kept to the purpose of resolving on a petition for the reform of Parliament. If nevertheless the speakers were arrested, the people had been told in advance not to resist. Not only that, but Hunt offered himself for arrest two days before the meeting, and the magistrates declined because he had done nothing illegal. They feared the worst, but felt they must await developments. They had both yeomanry and troops in readiness, but declined to summon General Byng, commander of the forces in the north, who was well experienced in such situations. The magistrates had also prepared a warrant for Hunt's arrest. On 16th August a great crowd, including many women and children, assembled in St. Peter's Fields in orderly fashion. It was reckoned by Hunt to number 150,000, but the estimate of Hulton, the chairman of the magistrates, was 60,000, and as this was supported by a prominent Radical observer it has been generally accepted. Nothing more provocative was displayed than banners, and Caps of Liberty hoisted on poles. The bands greeted Hunt's appearance by playing 'See the Conquering Hero Comes', 'God Save the King', and 'Rule Britannia'. The meeting had not been in progress for many minutes when the magistrates ordered the constables to seize Hunt, and the yeomanry, who had arrived before the regular soldiers, to support them. The yeomen had to reach the hustings from the edge of the dense crowd, and immediately used their sabres—whether the flat or the edge was disputed—to clear the way. They arrested the people on the hustings and then made to seize the banners of the contingents near by, again striking down those in their path. Then the regular troops, the hussars, were ordered in, and with the yeomen quickly cleared the whole area of people, pursuing some into the side streets. Eleven dead were picked up, including two women, and about 400 people were injured—wounded by sabres, trampled by horses, or thrown down and injured by the fleeing crowd.

This, in brief, is the account (based on Dr. Read's carefully documented study) that has been sifted from a large body of evidence. There were eye-witnesses, some Radical, some on the side of the magistrates, a few, including newspaper men, impartial. Evidence was given in the courts: at inquests, at the trial of Hunt (who was sentenced to two-and-a-half years' imprisonment) and in a test action brought later by one of the injured against the chairman of the magistrates. While it is virtually impossible to achieve certainty about the details of such an episode, on the whole the evidence of the Radicals who were present is borne out, the chief point being that violence was used by armed men, without provocation, against an orderly and peaceful crowd, who only later retaliated by throwing stones. A recent book, *Peterloo: The Case Reopened*, by Robert Walmsley (1969), seeks to prove by a reassessment of the evidence that other versions rely on a Radical concoction, that violence was first used *against* the yeomen, and that the magistrates had no choice but to take the action they did. Since no new evidence is produced in support of this view, the accepted account is likely to hold the field.

The Manchester magistrates received the approval of Lord Sidmouth and the special congratulations of the Regent. The government rejected a petition, signed by 6000 persons, condemning the action of the magistrates and asking for an official inquiry. Many people of moderate views were outraged by the violence that had been let loose on the demonstrators, and a most effective note of derision was contributed to the chorus of criticism by the Manchester newspaper which coined the word 'Peterloo' a few days after the event. The government maintained its unyielding attitude, which seemed to mean that in what was almost a state of war between the owners of property and the working class the country's rulers were committed to support of the one and repression of the other.

How had the catastrophe come to pass? The vast crowd which assembled in St. Peter's Fields was activated by working-class solidarity and by distress which only the government could relieve, and proclaimed that if this government would not, a reformed one must take its place. The Manchester magistrates were mainly cotton manufacturers and merchants (though a Church of England clergyman was prominent among them) determined to hold down the workpeople. The special constables and the yeomanry, formed in 1817, were recruited from the same class, with the addition of shopkeepers, no doubt anxious for the safety of their goods, and publicans, who joined to please the magistrates.

All these guardians of the peace were quite genuine in their fear of revolution, and never more so, probably, than when they beheld the great gathering in St. Peter's Fields, unarmed though it was. There is no evidence, however, that the magistrates let the meeting assemble in order to be able to break it up. Nor is there evidence in the Home Office papers that the government intended this to happen. E. P. Thompson, however, believes that it did: 'My opinion is: (a) the Manchester authorities intended to employ force; (b) Sidmouth knew and assented to their intention to arrest Hunt and disperse the crowd, but was unprepared for the violence with which it was effected.' But he adds, 'We shall never be able to determine with certainty whether or not Liverpool and Sidmouth were parties to the decision to use force.' Mr. Thompson refuses to give credence to the letters Sidmouth had sent restraining the magistrates from too hasty a resort to force, saying that they were written 'for the record'. It seems unlikely, however, that Tory ministers were so sensitive about the verdict of public opinion, since they obviously thought their policy right and necessary. On the main point—the complicity of the government—Mr. Thompson's opinion, as he admits, is unsupported by evidence. The government's congratulations to the magistrates, misconceived as they must seem, are not evidence of this kind. Public order throughout the country depended in the first instance on the promptitude in decision of local magistrates; if the government had turned round on the Manchester magistrates the authorities everywhere would have felt betrayed. As Canning said, 'To let down the magistrates would be to invite their resignation, and to lose all gratuitous service in the counties liable to disturbance for ever.' The government was genuinely concerned for the maintenance of public order, but preferred to secure it by traditional methods and without unnecessary resort to force. In the absence of a trained police force its policy was always likely to fail, as it did at Peterloo. But there is no proof, and little reason to suppose, that the government conspired with the magistrates to provoke, and then to crush, a great demonstration of the popular demand for reform.

4 After Peterloo Moderate opinion became more liberal as a result of Peterloo. Many people were revolted by violence of a kind which might be customary in Ireland, but which they thought foreign to English traditions. There were members of the middle class, even in Manchester itself, who were soon campaigning for the reform of local government that was so obviously needed and for representation in Parliament. Peel was to sense the changed atmosphere, and to respond to it with the first systematic reforms of the century. The government's immediate reaction was far different. The ministry armed itself for a new campaign of repression not only by adding 10,000 men to the Army, but by summoning a special session of Parliament to pass, in little more than a month, the Six Acts. To create public support for these extreme measures they relied on a general state of alarm in the country of which a flood of letters from worried magistrates provided ample evidence.

The first of the Acts prohibited assembly for drilling or other military exercises—a wholesome measure. The second made it illegal to possess or carry arms; this was introduced with some apology; it was temporary, and applied only to certain areas. The third Act, a long one, imposed further restrictions on the right, once regarded as fundamental, of public meeting. Attendance at a meeting was limited to residents of the parish where it was held; no meeting of any kind was allowed which would excite hatred of the government or the constitution. Two other Acts were directed against the Press, one providing severe penalties for publishing blasphemous or seditious libels, the other bringing under the stamp duty pamphlets and any other form of political comment, thus ending the evasion practised by Cobbett and others. The rumour of a project to charge duty on all the back numbers of *The Political Register* led to Cobbett's flight to the United States. The last of the Acts put an end to legal delays which might be used to the advantage of an accused person, but might also be used to harass him.

What was the attitude of the Whig Opposition, traditional guardian of the people's liberties, in the face of this attack on them? In a way the party's position was inglorious, because, as

Brougham admitted, had they been in office they would have felt obliged to pass measures similar to those of the Tories, while, being in opposition, they were free to criticise them. However, they steered a course which enabled them in some measure to maintain their traditions, and—what was very important at this dangerous juncture—to keep in contact with reforming opinion outside Parliament. Grey laid down the party line with promptitude after Peterloo: Radical violence and the abrogation by the Tories of constitutional safeguards were both to be deplored. The Whig leaders were genuinely worried by the prospect, which Peterloo seemed to threaten, of a division of the nation, with the lower orders supporting violent Radicalism while the upper classes resorted to despotic Toryism. In preventing this the Whigs might prevent revolution, and if at the same time the party found new confidence and attracted wider support, these would be a not unwelcome political bonus. The disorders of 1816-17 had seemed to paralyse the Opposition, but Peterloo had the contrary effect. The Whigs in Parliament protested vigorously against the action of the Manchester magistrates, and mustered 150 votes in the Commons in favour of a government inquiry. Outside Parliament the Whigs organised several county meetings of protest. The government dismissed Lord Fitzwilliam from the post of Lord Lieutenant of Yorkshire for presiding over the meeting there. When the Six Acts came before Parliament the Whigs criticised them in detail, forcing sixteen divisions in the Commons, and condemned those which encroached on freedom of meeting and of the Press, arguing that these were essential safety valves. They did not, however, totally oppose the Acts. They seemed more anxious about the possibility of a military dictatorship, and objected strongly to the increase in the size of the Army. A few of their more progressive leaders, Tierney, Lord John Russell and Lambton (later Lord Durham), wanted to forestall the Radicals by bringing in a moderate measure of parliamentary reform, but in general the Whigs maintained that if the government would reduce excessive expenditure and taxation distress would be relieved and Radical agitation would die away. A. Mitchell, in *The Whigs in Opposition, 1815-1830*, sums up the improved position of the Whigs thus: 'The Whigs had taken a view clearly distinct from that of the government, and had energetically placed that view before the public, so putting themselves in a strong position for protecting and even heading that section of public opinion most congenial to their views'—the middle-class liberals and Radicals, moderate men of property.

Now that the working-class Radicals were denied their chosen means of urging reform—mass meetings and petitions—the Radical press became even more important. Cobbett had blazed the trail with *The Political Register*; now many others followed him in defying the law, since a 4d stamp would put their papers beyond the means of their readers. They needed courage: the mere advocacy of universal suffrage might be regarded by the courts as sedition, and they faced severe penalties for evading the stamp duty. In defiance of the repressive measures of 1817, T. J. Wooler began to issue *The Black Dwarf*; Cartwright wrote for it, and it reported the speeches of Henry Hunt. It was Wooler who first saw the advantages to the popular movement of imitating the organisation of the Methodists, especially their class meetings. Wooler was sent to prison in 1820, but in the previous year the publication of *The Black Dwarf* had been taken over by Richard Carlile (1790-1843), who later founded the Rotunda, a great centre of London working-class Radicalism. Carlile declaimed against religion as well as against the government, so that Wilberforce's society for 'the Suppression of Vice' prosecuted him in the courts. He suffered two terms of imprisonment lasting nine years, but his brave defiance made a great impression on the public, especially as he was able to continue publishing while in prison. These and other Radicals, constantly harassed by fines and imprisonment until persecution slackened in 1830, maintained their attacks on government abuses and their campaign for the people's rights, and had a most important influence in keeping up the demand for reform and the morale of the working class during the years of repression. When Brougham said that the Press had come to rival the House of Commons, since nothing else could speak the sense of the people, he must have been referring to 'the Unstamped' as well as to the legal Press.

Despite the efforts of the Radical journalists the cause suffered a decline in 1820. This was due in the main not to repression but to an improvement in trade and employment—bearing out Cobbett's dictum, 'I defy you to agitate a man with a full stomach.' The capital was agitated nevertheless over the affair of Queen Caroline. George IV, when Prince Regent, had never been able to tolerate his wife, Caroline of Brunswick, and in 1814 had banished her from his court. He wanted to ensure that she should never reappear there by obtaining a divorce, a step that seemed to him imperative when he succeeded to the throne in 1820 and Caroline prepared to assert her rights as Queen. Liverpool and his colleagues, however, had every reason for avoiding the unsavoury revelations of a trial held in public, which were likely to be equally damaging to the King, to the Queen, and to the ministers, who would have to take responsibility for the proceedings. An attempt to buy off the Queen failed; Brougham, who was her adviser, dared not transmit the terms of the bargain, which involved the surrender of her royal rights and permanent residence abroad.

Far from contemplating such a retirement, Caroline returned to England from a six years' exile to assert her position as Queen. She arrived in June, 1820, the King's accession having taken place in January, and immediately became the centre of vociferous but well-organised demonstrations of popularity which kept London in a ferment for months. It seemed that the public had seized upon the Queen as a symbol of persecuted innocence which gave full scope for the general hatred of the King and the government. Caroline was ill suited to the part. Almost every step she took was foolish and irresponsible, and her conduct during her wanderings abroad had furnished all the evidence that a divorce court could require. The procedure recommended to the King by his ministers, however, under the threat of dismissal if they would not satisfy him, was a Bill of Pains and Penalties based upon the Queen's misdeeds, a divorce clause being included in it. This was introduced into the House of Lords, and involved a public hearing through which the charges against the Queen and her counter-charges against her husband were poured day by day into the ears of the British public. It is remarkable that the monarchy survived the process. The upshot was that the Bill passed the Lords by only nine votes and the government then dropped it. The King did not get his divorce, but eventually Caroline was persuaded to abandon her claim to full royal status. When the coronation took place she was refused entry to Westminster Abbey, and this time the crowd did not take her side. She died in 1821, and 'the affair of Queen Caroline' was soon forgotten.

It had not been without political importance. The reputation of the Liverpool ministry, through little fault of its own, sank to its lowest point. It was weakened by the resignation of Canning, who had been a friend of the Queen and had dissociated himself from the divorce proceedings. The Cabinet simply dared not make use of its new powers to silence the Press and prohibit mass meetings; as it was the ministers thought the country might be on the brink of revolution. Yet the storm blew over, and the Radicals earned no lasting profit from it. The Whigs in fact gained more in popularity; they had made full use of the opportunity to embarrass the government, and Lord John Russell estimated that 'the Queen's business' had 'done a great deal of good in renewing the old and natural alliance between the Whigs and the people'.

Another episode of 1820 had done something to repair the government's reputation by showing some justification for its repressive activity. A band of eleven men, led by Arthur Thistlewood, a Spencean, plotted to assassinate the entire Cabinet when its members were assembled at dinner in a private house. The Bank of England was to be seized and a provisional government set up. There was a spy among the conspirators who supplied them with arms, forwarded their plans, and then arranged their arrest while they were gathered in a stable-loft in Cato Street, in north-west London. They had hatched their plot partly in revenge for Peterloo, but it convinced many people there were real dangers to social order which the government must repress.

Further evidence of desperate extremism soon came from Scotland, though spies took a large part in fomenting it. In the course of a widespread strike of colliers a number of them at

Bonnymuir attacked a small body of soldiers, who easily captured several of their assailants. Trials and executions concluded the affair, which in its futility and hopelessness resembled the Pentrich Rising three years before.

5 How near to revolution?

Was Britain on the verge of a revolution in this period? Those who feared revolution at the time were undoubtedly influenced by the recollection of events in France in 1789. But in fact the differences between the two countries, in economic, social and political factors, are much more striking than the similarities. Indeed an examination of the two cases may suggest that the only common factors were the impact of economic disorder and consequent social distress. These had not been the sole cause of the Revolution in France. Were they likely to bring about a revolution in Britain without the operation of other causes? Were there countervailing influences to explain why revolution was avoided?

In 1817 and 1819 there was a conjunction of high prices, harsh conditions for the workers, and considerable unemployment. Of these it was probably the last which had the most to do with political agitation, for in years of fuller employment the workmen turned their pressure on the employers in an attempt to better their wages and conditions. More fundamental than these short-term factors was a degree of exploitation inseparable from the early stages of an industrial revolution because of the need to accumulate capital for further development rather than raise wages and so increase consumption expenditure. Hardship and misery were the unchanging lot of a large section of the wage-earners. But it was only in years of acute distress that unrest was at all widespread. When conditions improved the force went out of working-class protest, as the history of the movement for parliamentary reform, and later of the Chartist movement, makes plain. It was not likely that a revolutionary movement would gather momentum from the unaided impulse of social distress.

Some historians have judged nevertheless that Britain was ripe for revolution at this time, and in seeking to explain how it was avoided have emphasised the influence of religion. Their argument has been that the Nonconformists, especially the Methodists, taught the lower classes to practise submission to their superiors as well as to the will of God, to bear adversity without complaint, and to look to a future life for the only certain happiness. Thus quietened, the working class sought change by peaceful means, or did not seek it at all. As Charles Kingsley, the Christian Socialist, said later (followed by Karl Marx), 'Religion is the opium of the people.'

The best-known exponent of the view that Methodism saved England from revolution is Elie Halévy. Having examined, in his *History of the English People in the Nineteenth Century*, the political and economic systems, and found both lacking in the elements of stability and order, he then turns to religion and finds in it the answer to his central question: What was the secret of the nation's success in combining liberty with stability? His discussion (Vol. I, Part III, pp. 423-8) stresses, however, the influence of religion on the middle, not the working classes, for he believes that the leaders of a revolution could have come only from the middle class—leaders who would have provided the working classes with 'an ideal, a creed, and a definite programme of action'. Because the middle class was indoctrinated with religion it produced no such leaders, and therefore no revolution took place. So fascinated was Halévy by this argument that he omitted to prove the existence of an actual revolutionary situation, relying merely on Britain's archaic constitution and un-controlled economic development as likely causes of a revolution.

If the influence of religion on the working class is examined, there is much evidence to suggest that Methodism, so far from being an enervating influence, invigorated the working class by providing a training school for its leaders. Not only did the Methodists teach many people to read and write; the sect depended very much on lay preachers, who gained practice in public speaking, and developed organising ability and a sense of responsibility for their fellow men. Loveless, one of the Tolpuddle labourers sentenced in 1833, was a lay preacher, and had 'a small theological library' in his cottage. Methodists were prominent in the Luddite movement, in the campaign for parliamentary reform, and later in the Chartist movement. There is the further point that some of the political societies, the Hampden Clubs for example, deliberately copied Methodist organisation—mass meetings, weekly classes, penny-a-week contributions, central conference. This weighty, and perhaps essential, contribution of the sects to working class movements was recognised at the time by many observers.

E. P. Thompson, in *The Making of the English Working Class*, attacks from two directions the theory that religion held back the workers from revolutionary activity. In the first place, he points out that deists like Paine, Carlile and Owen had more influence on the working class than the sects, whose stronghold was the middle class. He believes (though precise figures cannot be ascertained) that the proportion of working men who were Methodists was too small for their influence to be decisive. He shows too that working men appeared 'most sober and disciplined, in the twenty years after the wars, when most in earnest to assert their rights', which suggests that the pursuit of definite objectives generated its own discipline. The restraint shown in the mass movements in Manchester, for example, cannot be traced to the influence of the sects.

Mr. Thompson suggests, secondly, that the teaching of the Methodists mainly took effect in a different direction. He points to the employers' need of a disciplined labour force, whether they engaged workers on the outwork system or employed them in factories. Wages were not good enough to induce the worker to give of his best; fear of dismissal might inhibit idleness but could not evoke responsibility and skill. Mr. Thompson quotes Ure's *Philosophy of Manufacturers* (1835) for the answer to the problem: 'It is . . . the interest of every mill-owner to organise his moral machinery on equally sound principles with his mechanical.' Little less than a transformation of human nature was required, and the sects went far to achieve it. According to Methodist teaching the gift of grace was not obtained once and for all, but had to be secured by 'service to the Church, religious exercises, and a disciplined life'. Work was itself virtuous; children from their earliest days were taught that idleness was sinful.

This was the creed that produced large numbers of obedient workers, expecting little from life and slow to complain of its injustices, and it is they who bear witness to what Mr. Thompson calls 'the transforming power of the Cross'. It is obviously difficult to support such a thesis by precise evidence, and if, as Mr. Thompson believes, the proportion of workers who belonged to the sects is too small to explain political quietism, is it not likewise too small to explain industrial discipline?

There would seem to be little substance left to support the theory that religious influence saved England from revolution. Halévy relied on the power of this influence on the middle class, which was in fact to be easily satisfied with the reform of Parliament in 1832, and which showed no really revolutionary tendencies. Among working class people Methodism was weak in numbers, and while it provided training for some of their leaders, it seems to have had only a limited effect as either a stimulating or a moderating factor. If the people were not restrained from revolt by religion—and no other restraining influence has been suggested—it would seem that the whole argument rests upon a false assumption, and that the country was never in fact on the verge of revolution.

Many people at the time, of course, feared an imminent revolt, which they believed, as did the government, was being prepared by a deliberate conspiracy. Castlereagh explained the disorders of 1816-17 as due to 'poisonous propaganda disseminated by men of culture and ability among the ignorant and suffering'. Against this it must be remembered that very few men were deliberately trying to engineer a revolution, certainly not those with the largest following, like Cobbett, Cartwright and Hunt. They were all bringing the government into disrepute, but they were trying to change its policies, and to reform, not subvert, the constitution. The Radicals and socialists were weakened by the diversity of their aims and their lack of cohesion. In general they had neither the will nor the ability to make a revolution, and therefore one must conclude that there was some degree of panic in the reaction of the ruling class to the disorders of this period.

6 Was there a counter-revolution?   Did this reaction amount
to a counter-revolution, as Mr. Thompson asserts when he
identifies (in Chap. VI) three influences of first importance in this
period: the rapid increase in population, the technical revolution
in industry, and 'political counter-revolution' lasting from 1792
to 1832? Halévy too speaks of a 'counter-revolutionary terror' in
1817. The government cannot of course be acquitted of the
charge of taking a completely negative attitude to the problems
of the time. It would not yield an inch on constitutional change, it
showed no interest in reform, and it made no attempt to deal
with economic problems—except to favour the landed interest.
'Are we', asked Castlereagh in December, 1819, 'to recognise the
policy of taking from one class merely for the purpose of giving
to another?' The ministers believed that intervention in economic
affairs was not only undesirable but impossible: Liverpool con-
tended, quite sincerely, that there was nothing the government
could do to alter the situation. Given the state of knowledge and
the administrative resources of the time, he was largely justified
in his belief.

If it be granted that there was little the government could do
to provide remedies for distress, was it unduly harsh in its
measures of repression? One consideration is so obvious that it
may be overlooked: the first duty of a government is to maintain
order. The means available to the British government in the early
nineteenth century were inadequate, and this meant that the consequences of any failure would be serious. At least the government
of Lord Liverpool showed determination to govern; the fall of the
French monarchy in 1789 had been partly caused by its failure to
do so. The question remains, however, whether the government
of 1815-22 behaved as the enemy of the mass of the people—
whether it engaged itself in a counter-revolution.

A strongly negative answer is given by both R. J. White and
Dr. N. McCord. The government, says Mr. White, in *From
Waterloo to Peterloo*, was not greatly preoccupied with disorder
and treason, nor was the House of Commons very interested; de-
bates on the spy system and even on the suspension of Habeas
Corpus were poorly attended. (This might be considered a double-

edged argument.) He agrees that Liverpool was alarmed by the way the lower classes were being organised by their leaders, but insists that he trusted (in his own words) in the 'gradual effect of the policy of the government', and believed in the traditional methods of keeping order. Evidence of this can be found in the government's grant of a million pounds in 1818 for the building of churches in the new towns, and perhaps also in the stipulation in one of the Six Acts that meetings should be confined to the residents of a parish—the parson and the squire were still, as in previous centuries, to keep their flock from straying.

Dr. McCord, in an article on 'The Government of Tyneside, 1800-1850' (*Transactions of the Royal Historical Society, 1970*), not only plays down the repressive element in government but also the disorder it was designed to curb. He suggests that agitation was largely ineffective, and finds, in a period of vast economic and social change, remarkably little conflict, violence or repression. He gives the credit to the authorities, central and local; he produces examples from Tyneside of concern for the hardships of the poor, of criticism of unreasonable employers, of magistrates as trusted mediators in strikes, and of officers of the Army and Navy behaving with sagacious moderation. It must be noted that some of his most impressive evidence comes from the 1830s rather than an earlier period, but this does not apply to the example quoted by Professor Briggs, which relates to 1819, the most troubled year of all. He points out that some magistrates—usually members of the squirearchy who had no liking for mill-owners—'showed sympathy and understanding. In a memorial sent to Sidmouth only a few weeks before Peterloo the magistrates of Salford Hundred emphasised "the deep distresses of the manufacturing class of this extensive population", and added, "When the people are oppressed with hunger we do not wonder at their giving ear to any doctrine which they are told will redress their grievance." '

These more optimistic views seem to leave too much out of account—the abrogation of freedom of meeting and freedom of the Press, Sidmouth's employment of spies, the fierce harshness of the penal system, 'the deadly seriousness' with which the government treated outbreaks of disorder. Forgotten also are the large number of troops—the majority of the 23,000 maintained in Great Britain—posted to the industrial areas, and the new barracks being built to house them.

One is left with the dominant impression of a ruling class convinced that the lower orders must be kept in their place, and that any attempt on their part to leave it must be treated as dangerous insubordination. This reverence for a hierarchical society also showed itself, however, in a preference for a traditional social discipline, administered by local authorities without armed force, and in reluctance to push repression to the limit. A government really bent on counter-revolution would have produced not one Peterloo but many, death sentences by the hundred rather than the dozen, and transportation for thousands rather than a few hundreds of victims.

One is impelled also to wonder that people brought up in often sordid surroundings, with little or no education, and no strangers to violence in everyday life, should have pinned their hopes on constitutional reform and have campaigned for it over long periods and large areas without violence of any kind. Perhaps Francis Place was right when he said that the campaign itself had 'elevated the character of the working man'. While the country's rulers, as the immediate sequel to Peterloo shows, were not favourably impressed at first by the discipline of the people, it may have helped to move them towards a posture of negotiation rather than repression, and so contributed to the opening of an era of reform in the 1820s.

Chapter IV

Towards Reform

1 A policy for prosperity From 1822 the rule of the Tories took on a different complexion, so that, though Lord Liverpool still presided and made no sweeping changes in the Cabinet, the 1820s came to be known as the era of the 'Liberal Tories'. How real was the change from the period of repression that had gone before? There was certainly no decision by Liverpool and his colleagues to adopt a new line of policy; still less was the Tory party in general converted to reform. There was perhaps a milder temper in its ranks as the memory of the French Revolution receded, but more important were the changes which brought men of special ability and forceful character into some of the key posts in government. It was recognised by them, if not by the party in general, that a wider basis of support must be found, for as a result of the agricultural depression the country gentry in the Commons were restive and their Tory loyalty more dubious than ever. If this support was to come from the men of business, who were obviously becoming more important to the nation, the government must show a better understanding of their problems than the Tories had done hitherto. These various factors together, with an impetus sometimes added by unforeseen events, produced enough in the way of progressive achievement to distinguish these from the previous years of Tory rule, though in allocating the credit here it must be noted that to enact their major reforms ministers would have to depend on the support of the Whigs.

The problems which, apart from foreign affairs, first required the government's attention were economic and financial. There was a sharp fall in agricultural prices despite the Corn Law of 1815, which in any case had been found to work badly. Although the output of manufactured goods was increasing, the prospects for trade were uncertain, and in many districts there was distress. A return to the gold standard in 1821 did not bring the security or the prosperity that had been expected. In periods of unrest public order was obviously insecure, and likely to remain so while the traditional means of enforcement were relied on.

In the face of these difficulties the government had cut a poor figure in the House of Commons, where the Cabinet was represented only by Castlereagh, who was by no means eloquent, and four rather undistinguished colleagues. As Peel's friend Croker put it, 'A government cannot go on without the gift of the gab.' A series of changes now gave new strength to the ministerial team. Early in 1822, Liverpool brought in Peel as Home Secretary and allowed Sidmouth to retire to a less active post. When in August of the same year Castlereagh, exhausted by overwork and strain, took his own life, Liverpool filled the vacancy at the Foreign Office by appointing Canning, with whom he had always been on good terms since their Oxford days. Canning was much the most brilliant figure among the Tories, and a more effective Leader of the House than Castlereagh. In the conduct of foreign policy the difference in style, if not in policy, was marked; in Halévy's words, 'A poet had succeeded the man of prose.' Canning contrived to persuade the Tories that he was continuing the sound and cautious policy of Castlereagh, and at the same time to convince liberals at home and abroad that he was the friend of progress and popular rule.* Early in 1823 Vansittart, whose ten years at the Treasury had brought no notable achievement, was replaced by Robinson, who was succeeded at the Board of Trade by Huskisson. Both recognised that a new Britain was evolving in which trade and industry must play a larger part, and in their measures to advance commercial prosperity they had the backing

* For the foreign policy of Canning *see* D. R. Ward, *Foreign Affairs 1815-1865* in this series

of the Prime Minister. After these changes seven of the former Cabinet ministers remained, notably Eldon as Lord Chancellor and Wellington as Master-General of Ordnance, but with the recent reinforcement Liverpool could congratulate himself on having brought together most of the surviving 'friends of Mr. Pitt'.

In economic and financial affairs the reigning principles were those of Adam Smith's *The Wealth of Nations* (published in 1776), and their foremost exponent was David Ricardo (1772-1823), who made a fortune on the Stock Exchange and later entered Parliament. The government therefore leaned towards free trade, while committing itself to a sound money policy which pleased the financiers but antagonised the landowners. The choice was between an elastic currency which could be adjusted to expanding trade, and a medium of exchange which should be absolutely fixed and reliable. The former meant leaving discretion to the banks, or at least to the Bank of England, to regulate the issue of notes; the latter meant a return to the old practice, suspended during the wars, whereby gold coin formed the staple currency, and notes could at any time be exchanged for gold. In 1819 a committee presided over by Peel reported in favour of the gold standard, and in 1821 the Bank of England acted on the recommendation, paying out gold on request in return for notes, except for those of low values. This did not cause all paper money to go out of circulation, and it is by no means certain that the total currency was reduced. But whatever the cause, there was a marked fall in prices that began in late 1820 and continued in 1821. In the case of corn there was no mystery about the reason. There was a bumper harvest in 1820, and the price of wheat, despite the total prohibition of imports under the law of 1815, fell to 41s 6d a quarter. The landowners clamoured for relief. They wanted a sliding scale of duties on imports, rising as the price fell below 80s, but starting even above that figure; they demanded a reduction of taxes, and they argued most emphatically of all for a depreciation of the currency, i.e. a deliberate increase in the amount of money in circulation in order to raise prices. This last remedy was barred by Huskisson and Ricardo, but eventually the government saw the need of some concession to the country gentlemen in Parliament, whom the Whigs were trying to attract into their camp, and in 1822 the Act of 1815 was repealed. Imports would be allowed when the home price was 70s (as against 80s previously) but would have to pay a duty of 12s; the duty would be reduced to 5s when the price exceeded 80s and to 1s only when it rose above 85s. None of this was to take effect until the price again reached 80s. This in fact it never did. so the landed interest gained nothing. In contrast to 1815, Lord Liverpool was now prepared to tell the landowners that they must look mainly to an improvement of the market to solve their troubles. He even pointed out to them the benefit of low prices to the poor. By 1825 the agricultural depression was over, and in any case a succession of government changes then deferred any alteration of the corn law.

An even more emphatic change of outlook marked the trade policy of the government. William Huskisson (1770-1830) declared the need for 'a full and complete revision of our commercial system'. As a young man Huskisson had served in the British Embassy in Paris, and like Lord Liverpool had witnessed the capture of the Bastille in 1789. In 1796 he had entered Parliament, and later was member for Liverpool, and therefore in close touch with commercial interests. In office from 1814, he became familiar with every aspect of the economy, and for some years he was the government spokesman on agricultural questions. He supported the Corn Law of 1815, but later changed his mind and became completely opposed to the prohibition of imports. This apparent desertion of the cause of the landowners caused serious disagreements with other ministers and aroused the hostility of the country gentlemen in the House of Commons. In financial and business circles, on the other hand, Huskisson was highly respected, and he had their support for the steps he now took to reform the whole policy of the government in respect to trade and shipping. The basis of Huskisson's reforms was his belief in freer trade, and he was able to take great strides in this direction because the country had progressed so far in the new methods of manufacture that the network of protective regulations which may formerly have been useful was no longer needed.

British businessmen could usually undersell their rivals both at home and abroad, and British shipping could secure its share of the world's rapidly growing trade without the help of the navigation laws.

The revision of the Navigation Acts, which dated mainly from the seventeenth century, had been recommended by a committee of the House of Commons in 1822, and had actually been begun before Huskisson became President of the Board of Trade. The object of the Acts had been to reserve to England the trade with her colonies and the shipping of goods bound for England across the oceans, while special restrictions had been aimed at the Dutch, once the chief carriers for Europe. Now the restrictions on trade with Europe were removed, except for certain enumerated articles, provided that other governments would concede similar terms. British trade with non-European countries was still barred to European carriers, but the new states of North and South America were allowed to share in it—a change which assisted the rapid growth of the U.S. merchant fleet—and while trade between Britain and her colonies must still be carried in British or colonial ships, the colonies' trade with foreign countries was freed from almost all restrictions. Thus the ports of British colonies in America were opened to U.S. shipping, and the British colonies were free to export their produce direct to Europe and Africa, instead of sending it all to Britain as they had previously been obliged to do. In the course of these changes what had become an impenetrable tangle of regulations was simplified and clarified. The repeal of so much of the old Navigation Laws did Britain no harm. The shipping lines flourished on competition, particularly because Britain was soon to take the lead in building iron ships driven by steam power. Nor did the Navy suffer from the repeal of laws intended partly to secure its supply of man-power, for it now trained its own crews instead of relying on recruits, mostly unwilling, from the merchant navy.

An attack of at least equal vigour was launched against the direct regulation of commerce by duties and prohibitions. In 1820 a notable petition had been organised in the City of London, asking Parliament for a new trade policy. Its central statement set forth pure laissez-faire doctrine: 'The maxim of buying in the cheapest market and selling in the dearest, which regulates every merchant in his individual dealings, is strictly applicable as the best rule for the trade of the whole nation.' A policy based on this principle would enrich every state; Britain should get other nations to abandon their restrictive practices by setting them an example. The business community had been stimulated to make this move, remarkably enough, by members of the government, particularly Liverpool and Robinson. It was therefore promptly followed up by action, which first took the form of reciprocal treaties. By an Act of Parliament of 1823 the government was given power to conclude treaties with foreign states whereby duties on goods and shipping entering British ports would be reduced in return for similar concessions granted by the other country. In the next few years reciprocity treaties were signed with most of the European states—mainly to Britain's advantage, because her output was greater than that of any rival.

Many other steps were taken towards freeing trade without waiting for reciprocal action abroad. The silk industry had been favoured with a complete prohibition of imports. This was now replaced by a duty of 30%—causing in this case serious difficulties for the industry. The same policy was followed with a wide range of articles; prohibitions, or duties so high as to be prohibitive, were replaced by duties no higher than 30%, and in many cases lower. It was calculated that a duty of 30% made smuggling unprofitable, or at least not worth the risk; certainly this once lucrative occupation was never the same again after Huskisson. The wholesale reduction of duties encountered no opposition from Robinson, Chancellor of the Exchequer, because they had been so high that there were few lawful imports to pay them. The position was different with duties on imported raw materials, which had been imposed purely to obtain revenue. These Huskisson abolished because they handicapped the manufacturer. Bounties on exports were discontinued or greatly reduced because no such stimulus to production was any longer needed. All this work on the regulation of trade was crowned, as with the Navigation Acts, by a codification of the law. A single tariff for the whole of the United Kingdom replaced over a thousand Customs Acts previously in force.

While reducing duties Huskisson retained and improved the system of imperial preference by permitting the import of colonial products at lower rates than foreign. The duty on foreign sugar remained so high that West Indian sugar had a monopoly of the British market, while still subject to a duty high enough to account for a third of the total yield from customs. The rate for Canadian timber was so much lower than that for Baltic timber that it sometimes paid a Norwegian exporter to ship his timber to Canada and pass it off as a colonial product. There were preferences likewise on wheat, wool and silk from countries of the Empire. In this way almost every colony received some benefit, and was of course required in return to admit British goods at a lower rate of duty than those of foreign countries. It is plain, therefore, that Huskisson, while doing so much to free external trade, did not believe in total laissez-faire, for he made use of preferences in a systematic policy of imperial development, perhaps conceiving of an Empire that should one day be self-sufficient. But after his time it was the ideal of free trade that flourished, and imperial preference had gradually to be sacrificed to it.

The new trend in commercial policy was strongly supported by the diplomacy of Canning, a close friend of Huskisson and M.P. for Liverpool, where mercantile interests were dominant. Canning regarded the promotion of trade as a major function of foreign policy. The prospects of British merchants in South America, exaggerated though they may have been, were an important reason for his recognition of the new republics arising from the ashes of the Spanish Empire. Trade in the Eastern Mediterranean also was valuable, and must be protected from the possibility of the disruption of the Ottoman Empire or of domination of the region by a rival Power. The problem of Greek independence was solved in such a way that these dangers were averted.

On the home front Huskisson's policy received warm support from Robinson as Chancellor of the Exchequer, as well as from

Liverpool himself. Robinson, compared with Vansittart, who had 'asked no more of the House of Commons than a blind faith in the mystic rites of which he was the attendant priest', seemed for a time to be brilliantly successful. He achieved a substantial reduction of expenditure (though this had been begun in 1821-22 owing to the pressure of Joseph Hume, the Radical M.P.) and consequently, through the insistence of the House of Commons, in taxation. He was materially aided by the gradual recovery of trade from the depression which had smitten the country so severely in 1819. In his first Budget speech in 1823—a very able exposition which made his parliamentary reputation—Robinson forecast a period of prosperity, and pleased the House of Commons by removing or reducing many of the 'assessed taxes'—direct taxes on carriages and servants, for example, which fell mainly on the rich. He justified this by claiming that the benefits thus dispensed would filter down through tradespeople and others to reach the mass of the population. In 1824, however, when he was able to declare a surplus, he helped the poor more directly by cancelling many taxes on commodities, among them coal, wool and rum, and in 1825 he remitted the house and window taxes on smaller houses, as well as implementing Huskisson's plans for a widespread reduction of customs duties. At the same time the internal system of collection was completely overhauled and greatly improved. All classes received some benefit from the Chancellor's measures; the scaling down of duties and prohibitions helped the expansion of trade, and the optimism of Robinson himself contributed to the general cheerfulness of the business world, though it was Cobbett who dubbed him—ironically—'Prosperity Robinson'. The irony seemed deserved when the next year, 1826, brought another trade slump, a fall in revenue, and consequently a much less cheerful Budget.

2 Peel at the Home Office   Robert Peel was deeply involved in all three of the foremost political questions of the 1820s—'Cash, Corn and Catholics'. The first two were decisively affected by his work on the committee of inquiry into the currency in 1819. Of the third he had earlier gained experience as Chief Secretary for

Ireland from 1812 to 1818, and he was to play a dramatic part in its later development. But meanwhile he entered on a relatively uncontroversial phase of his career as Secretary of State for Home Affairs (1822-1827 and 1828-30), a post in which he brought to bear his lucid and powerful intellect, his immense capacity for work and his experience of administration, especially of maintaining law and order in Ireland.

In the ten years 1811-21 there had been a steady and alarming increase in crime which the police, the prisons and the penal law were utterly unfitted and inadequate to deal with. The only remedies attempted by Parliament during the past fifty years had been the enactment of the death penalty for a large variety of offences, to a total of about two hundred, and, for crimes considered a little less serious, the substitution of transportation to Australia for imprisonment. The wholesale prescription of capital punishment was due not simply to vindictiveness but to an anxious concern for property and to sheer desperation: so few criminals were caught that savage punishment was inflicted as an alternative deterrent. It was quite ineffective. When shoplifting was punished by hanging, the shopkeeper often failed to prosecute, witnesses to testify, the jury to convict, and the Crown to confirm the sentence. Of those condemned to death only one in twenty was executed; in shoplifting cases the proportion was one in 1200. The offender thus had so good a chance of escaping punishment that he was not deterred; if the death penalty was to be at all effective the number of capital offences must be reduced.

The rest of the penal system was equally irrational and ineffectual, and at the same time utterly debasing. Various forms of corporal punishment were practised, even on women. The state of the prisons was appalling. They were terribly overcrowded, and their inmates often included lunatics, diseased persons, and children from nine upwards. On the other hand fees were paid to the keeper of the prison, and there were various amenities for those who could afford them, so that the prison system achieved the maximum of squalor but not always the maximum of deterrence. The alternative to a long prison sentence was transportation, and while a peer, arguing for the death penalty, said transportation meant 'a summer airing by an easy migration to a milder climate', his description is not borne out by accounts of the voyage to Australia and the subsequent treatment of the convicts.

Impulses to reform came from several quarters, the basic ideas having been provided in the eighteenth century by thinkers of the Enlightenment, notably Montesquieu, Beccaria and Rousseau. Many lawyers were worried by the absurdities of the English penal system, and there was Bentham's system of doctrine as a framework for reform. Quakers and Evangelicals made reform of the prisons one of the most urgent of their tasks, and Radical M.P.s were their allies in a long campaign. It was uphill work; owners of property in general, as well as judges and politicians, feared that any relaxation of the law would unleash uncontrollable violence. Three times Bills introduced by Romilly to abolish the death penalty for minor offences were passed by the Commons but rejected by the House of Lords. Sir John Mackintosh, the Whig M.P. who led the campaign after Romilly's death, succeeded in getting a committee of inquiry appointed, but it had only one immediate result—the theft of goods from a shop would incur the death penalty only if their value was fifteen pounds or more, instead of five shillings.

When Peel came into office he accepted most of the findings of this committee, but took the reform process entirely into his own hands. He proceeded with his usual caution; he consulted the judges about all major changes, and of course Eldon, still Lord Chancellor, had to be persuaded of their necessity, a process which seems to have been assisted by Peel's new standing in the Tory party. Peel believed that if new penal laws were forced upon the courts they would be badly administered; it was better to go slowly. But he consulted Jeremy Bentham, who had proffered copious advice, in person; the colloquies of the doctrinaire philosopher and the realist statesman must have been interesting. In 1823 Acts were passed, with little opposition, to abolish the death penalty for more than a hundred offences, some of which Peel had added to the proposals of the reformers. Theft from a dwelling-house of goods worth less than five pounds, for example, was no longer a capital crime. A great many offences still carried the death penalty, and the reformers were far from satisfied. But Peel did not want to rush ahead of public opinion, and preferred to rely on the Crown's power of reprieve, exercised through the Home Secretary.

If in many cases imprisonment was to take the place of hanging, something must be done about the prisons. Accordingly the Gaols Act of 1823 established a prison in every county and in each of several large towns, to be administered by local magistrates and maintained out of local rates. Justices of the Peace were to inspect the prisons at least three times each quarter and report to Quarter Sessions, and they must also send a general report every year to the Home Office. To ensure that the same system of discipline should be enforced in all these prisons detailed regulations were drawn up, and they were later applied to prisons in the smaller towns. Some attention was paid to medical and even educational provision, and there were elaborate rules for the separation of prisoners into different categories, so that children, or people with contagious diseases, were no longer liable to be thrown in with the rest. Some of the worst horrors of the prison system were thus ended, but Peel did not hope for too much. 'The real truth is', he wrote, 'the number of convicts is too overwhelming for the means of proper and effectual punishment.'

Peel undertook also a much-needed simplification of criminal law. Many offences punishable by imprisonment with hard labour had come to be tried by magistrates without a jury. This was stopped in the course of reducing to one statute 85 Acts concerning the empanelling of juries. Similarly the procedure of the criminal courts was improved and a mass of criminal law reduced to order. On the subject of theft, which accounted for six-sevenths of all criminal charges, there were 92 statutes. These were condensed into a single enactment of thirty pages—a rationalisation to delight the heart of Bentham—and so began a process which was finally to transform the English criminal law.

The most essential reform, however, was the creation of an effective police force. This was very much Peel's personal achievement, for the reformers were not very interested in it, and he had to overcome strong opposition in Parliament; when he moved in 1822 for a select committee on the police of London the House rejected the proposal out of hand. Lovers of the old order regarded a police force as unnecessary—a remarkable opinion in the circumstances—while Radicals and liberals feared it as a weapon in the hands of a reactionary government. The Metropolitan Police Bill was introduced into Parliament only in 1829 after Peel's return to office, when thanks to his skilful management it went through with little opposition.

The new police force was to be established only in London (a special boundary being drawn to give a radius of ten miles) but it was Peel's hope that the example would be followed all over the country. The metropolis, with a population of a million and a half, had had, apart from the City, only 400 policemen, serving under the direction of the Home Secretary. They were of poor quality and expected extra fees for many of the duties they performed; they did not count as one of them the prevention, as opposed to the detection, of crime. Parishes sometimes engaged their own police, as did private persons and organisations. Under the terms of Peel's Act a force of a thousand men was newly recruited. The whole force was under the authority of the Home Secretary and was controlled by two new magistrates (soon renamed Commissioners) who were responsible for recruitment, training and discipline, while a Receiver was appointed as financial officer; funds came from special parish rates levied by the overseers of the poor. Peel's original appointments to the key posts were excellent, and the three worked as a harmonious team for twenty years, by which time the force was securely established. The training of the police stressed the importance of the prevention of crime and of good relations with the public. There was occasional trouble with London mobs in the early years, but the police found effective ways of dealing with it, and soon became generally popular. Their reputation enhanced that of Peel himself, and as in the next twenty-five years similar forces were established in many parts of the country, he could claim much of the credit for the fact that there was no repetition of Peterloo.

3 Financial and industrial problems The year 1825 brought a financial crisis and the beginnings of another trade depression. Several small banks failed, mainly through the excessive issue of notes, the total of which had nearly doubled in two years, and as a result of their exceptional drawings the reserves of the Bank of England itself fell from £14 million to £3.5 million. There had been an excess of speculative investment abroad, especially in Latin America, where Mexican mining was the latest attraction. The boom was followed, as before, by a slump. Many merchants were in difficulties, and business activity in general was slowed down. The government refused any direct assistance; Lord Liverpool said as usual that there was little it could usefully do, and that people must learn to be more cautious. The Bank of England was, however, allowed to furnish loans up to £3 million, and gradually confidence was restored and the Bank's own bullion replenished.

Fortunately the government saw the need nevertheless to reform the banking system. Private banks were restricted by being forbidden to print notes of values under five pounds. On the other hand it was made legal for the first time by the Bank Act of 1826 for new joint-stock banks to be founded, the monopoly previously enjoyed by the Bank of England being now limited to the region around London with a radius of 65 miles. The change was partly due to a persistent campaign by a Newcastle merchant, Thomas Joplin, who knew from experience that in Scotland joint-stock banks were both useful and sound. Many English banks were now put on a firmer basis, and a gradual process of amalgamation made them stronger still. The Bank of England at the same time was empowered to set up branches in the provinces, so that altogether there was a great improvement in facilities for commercial enterprise.

These were long-term benefits. Meanwhile the slump of 1826 was even more severe than those of 1816 and 1819. Its effects were aggravated by the fact that at the same time as the prices of manufactured goods fell, with wages reduced and workers stood off, food prices reached their peak. There was a flood of petitions asking for cheap bread, while rioting and machine-breaking were reported from many parts of the country. The government's response was different from that of 1819. Peel said, 'The great cause of apprehension is not in the disaffection but in the real distress of the manufacturing districts. There is as much forbearance as it is possible to expect from so much suffering.' The government was even prepared to take steps to relieve the situation. In the ports of Liverpool and Hull, close to the areas of the worst distress, large stocks of corn were held. Bills were hurried through Parliament to permit their release on payment of only a small duty, and to allow the import for a short period of a quantity of foreign corn. For the passage of these measures the government had to rely on Whig votes, since many of its own supporters blamed Huskisson's lowering of tariff barriers for the trade recession, while the country gentlemen in Parliament were doubly indignant, first about the deflationary effect of restricting the note issue, and now about the release of corn from bond. Tierney, speaking for the Whigs in the Commons, claimed—with considerable exaggeration—'Though the gentlemen opposite are in office, we are in power.'

Two years earlier the economic expansion of the early 1820s and the milder attitude of the government had made possible a reform which would have been frozen in the harsh climate of 1826 if it had been longer postponed. This was the repeal of the Combination Acts of 1799 and 1800, which were now condemned for the same reasons as restrictions on trade—that they were pernicious in principle and ineffectual in practice. Inspired by the fear of revolution prevailing during the wars, they forbade all combinations of workmen to exact higher wages or better conditions; corresponding restrictions on employers were included but were never enforced. The Acts were really superfluous, except for rapid action to break a strike. The right to trade had long been established at common law, and any act against an employer could be construed as an interference with this right, and therefore as a conspiracy, which would incur heavy penalties. The Combination Acts, by contrast, provided only for summary trial without a jury before two magistrates, which meant that the penalty was limited to three months' imprisonment. Proceedings in magistrates' courts were not recorded, and there has therefore been dispute as to how far the Acts were enforced. It may be that most prosecutions were still brought in the High Court, and that the Acts were little used. They were not very difficult to evade, since a trade union could be disguised as a friendly society or trade club, while in Scotland, because of differences in the legal system, they were a dead letter from the start. Nevertheless the Combination Acts were particularly unfair. There had been numerous laws, some dating back to the reign of Elizabeth I, providing for the regulation of wages by Justices of the Peace—a safeguard for the worker, in theory at least, in times of rising prices, and the existence of this safeguard had been held to justify the banning of trade unions. Parliament had swept away all these laws by 1814 in the interests of free trade—and the employers' profits—yet trade unions were still illegal. The argument against them was, of course, that they hindered free competition: the price of labour, as of everything else, should be determined by supply and demand.

The champions of the working classes rather surprisingly accepted this argument. Abolish the Combination Laws, they said, and the workman would cease to complain of the tyranny of his employer, and would realise that his wages were determined by the laws of economics. Master and man would co-operate to advance the prosperity of both; strikes and unrest would be a thing of the past. This Benthamite reasoning might seem obvious to the Radicals, but it was by no means certain to convince the Tories in the House of Commons. The campaign had to be planned with considerable skill, which was supplied in the customary way by Francis Place. He had been at work since 1814 compiling a mass of evidence. He had also prepared a large body of witnesses—working men of the most respectable type and also a number of employers—to testify to a committee of the House of Commons. The committee was hand-picked by Joseph Hume, Place's chief collaborator, its main concern being to prepare a Bill to permit the emigration of skilled workers, previously forbidden by statute. A clause repealing the Combination Acts, and also barring prosecution for conspiracy, was inserted in this

Bill, but received little attention from either House when the Bill was passed. Thus, in a fit of absence of mind, Parliament restored to workmen the right to form trade unions.

The results soon contradicted the forecasts of the Benthamites. Repeal was followed by a double outbreak of strikes, first to gain higher wages while trade was improving, then to resist reductions when the depression began. Parliament repented of its unwitting generosity, and in 1825 passed another Act to modify the first. Peel and Huskisson wanted very severe restrictions now to be put on the trade unions, but thanks to another great lobbying effort by Francis Place the new Combination Act was surprisingly moderate. Even Peel said in a debate, 'Men who have no property except their manual strength ought to be allowed to confer together . . . for the purpose of determining at what rate they will sell their property', though he would have emphasised the word 'confer'. So the right of combination was preserved, and unions could operate in the open, but in order to ensure the peaceful character of their activity a clause of the Act prohibited not only intimidation but 'molestation' and 'obstruction'. This made it very difficult to enforce a strike, for picketing to prevent men from going in to work could easily be represented as molesting or obstructing. So finally the government conceded little, but hoped that the labouring classes, pacified by the concession, would refrain from disorder and violence.

4 The Tories divided All the economic problems of the time—the currency, the corn laws, tariffs—had sown division in the Tory ranks. In the background, kept there as long as possible because of its dangers, was the most divisive question of all—Catholic emancipation. In addition there were personal antagonisms within the Cabinet which all Lord Liverpool's conciliatory skill could hardly prevent from developing into open rupture. In February 1827 Liverpool was incapacitated by a stroke, and a new Prime Minister had to be found. No one else proved able to hold together the diverse elements of the Tory party to present a united front to the nation. W. R. Brock claimed too much for Lord Liverpool when, on the strength of the five years of reforming activity from 1822 to 1827, he described him as 'one of the architects of the nineteenth century'. But his achievement was not negligible. Seeing his function perhaps as bringing and holding together all the former followers of William Pitt, he had provided a stable government at a time when the Opposition promised no real alternative. He had gathered together a group of ministers with liberal views on trade and had supported their reforms. He had backed Peel in his work at the Home Office and defended Canning when he was criticised for venturesome policies abroad. If his own equipment was little more than that of an experienced administrator, he employed it in his general supervision over the departments of government. In the difficult post-war years it may have been to the country's advantage to have a Prime Minister who was an administrator rather than an ardent party leader or political adventurer.

It was the latter description that some people would have applied to George Canning, who was to succeed Liverpool as Prime Minister. He had been Leader of the House of Commons as well as Foreign Secretary since 1822, and sometimes gave the impression that he was Prime Minister as well. His reputation of being the foremost of the Liberal group in the Cabinet he owed almost entirely to his conduct of foreign policy, for his 'guarded approval' of popular revolts abroad was not reflected in his views on reform at home. While Huskisson was his close friend and always received his support, economic affairs claimed little of his interest or attention. He had always spoken in defence of repressive measures in 1816-20, and still equated discontent with disaffection. He was opposed to reform of the Poor Law, and, not yielding even to Wellington in admiration of the British constitution, was firmly set against any change in the electoral system. Only on Catholic emancipation did he take the side of reform, and in so doing separated himself from Peel and incurred the hostility of the 'anti-Catholic' Tories in the Cabinet. What earned him the disapproval of his colleagues, however, was not merely disagreement on matters of policy, nor even his unconcealed dislike for the landowning class and his waspish tongue. It was his self-centredness, his confident belief that he was indispensable, and his calculated courting of popularity. For example, he publicised his efforts to stop other countries pursuing the slave trade, and liked to project himself as the Liberal hero confronting the villainous Metternich. He sought support for his policy outside Parliament by publishing his dispatches, and by using the Press and the platform to reach a wider audience, in a way that his colleagues found both novel and disagreeable. Most irksome of all was his success: the public was well aware of the disagreements in the Cabinet, and so gave Canning most of the credit for liberal measures while blaming the reactionaries for the government's failures.

On the retirement of Liverpool the choice of Prime Minister really rested between Canning and Wellington. Through his charm and the success of his foreign policy Canning had fully recovered the King's favour. Moreover, George IV did not like Wellington, and suspected a plot to force a high Tory ministry upon him. So it was Canning whom he invited to take office as head of the government. Six ministers immediately resigned, among them Wellington and Peel, both motivated by distrust of Canning, and Peel also by his objection to Catholic emancipation, which Canning favoured. Weakened by these Tory desertions, Canning was obliged to offer a share in government to the Whigs. Despite the disapproval of Grey, Lord Lansdowne and Tierney responded. It was a poor bargain for them: Canning got the support he could hardly do without, but in return the Whigs had only three ministries, no say in the distribution of patronage, no guarantee of Catholic emancipation, and of course no promise of parliamentary reform. The solution of the Catholic problem Canning certainly hoped to achieve, but this was denied him. He had been in poor health for some time, and in August 1827, after only six months as Prime Minister, he died. In July he had been able to announce the last of his triumphs in foreign policy—the Treaty of London, whereby Britain, Russia and France would compel the Sultan, if necessary, to accept their joint arbitration of his quarrel with his Greek subjects.* Canning died at the height

* For the foreign policy of Canning *see* D. R. Ward, *Foreign Affairs 1815-1865* in this series

of his popularity, honoured abroad as the champion of liberal causes, and presiding at home over the first government of a generally liberal colour since the death of Charles James Fox in 1807. In his political thinking, however, he was still the disciple of William Pitt, and it is doubtful whether he could have come to terms with the Britain of the Industrial Revolution, as Peel was to do.

Canning was succeeded briefly by Robinson, who at Canning's request had gone to the House of Lords as Lord Goderich to lead for the government there, thus alienating many of his Tory friends, who had been hostile to Canning. Goderich formed his ministry from the same elements as Canning's, though the Whigs served reluctantly under a leader who completely lacked Canning's prestige. On the insistence of George IV he appointed as Chancellor of the Exchequer Herries, a Tory who had withdrawn from Canning's ministry. Herries soon objected to what he thought was a plot by Huskisson to undermine his authority at the Treasury, and when Goderich went to report these difficulties to the King he suddenly found himself dismissed—before his ministry had even faced Parliament. This was for him the end of eighteen years continuously in office; intelligent, modest and well-liked by everyone, he was perhaps too kind and amiable for the highest places in government.

Having tried a weak Prime Minister the King now reconciled himself to accepting a strong one, and summoned Wellington. The Duke might have accepted less readily than he did if he could have foreseen the events of the next three years. He formed a ministry not unlike the last of Liverpool's. The Whigs of course went out, but the Canningite group of Liberal Tories remained, and Peel returned to lead the House of Commons and crown his work at the Home Office by the formation of the Metropolitan Police. The first problem for the new Cabinet was a modification of the corn duty, a Bill drafted by Huskisson during Canning's ministry having been wrecked by Wellington's amendments in the House of Lords. The Bill that now emerged from a tussle in the Cabinet was less liberal, but it was some improvement on the law of 1815 and the abortive attempt of

1822. Its main feature was again a sliding scale: when the price of wheat was 54s or lower the duty was prohibitive; between 54s and 66s the duty went down by a shilling for every shilling rise in the price; above 66s the grower was thought not to need much protection, so from 66s to 73s the duty went down by larger steps, until at 73s wheat came in free. This was far from the real freeing of the corn trade which Huskisson had aimed at, and like the 1815 law it worked badly, because dealers would hold wheat off the market and send up the price so that a lower rate of duty should operate. In this way scarcity was artificially contrived, and the farmers' plans were still bedevilled by a continuing fluctuation in prices.

The wrangle over the duty made bad blood between Wellington and Huskisson, but it was another matter that led to the early removal from the government of the Liberal Tories. In 1821 there had been an isolated case, under an Act of 1809, of the disfranchisement of a borough for corruption. In 1828 Penryn in Cornwall and East Retford in Nottinghamshire were similarly convicted. The Huskisson group wanted both seats to be transferred to Manchester, which was unrepresented in Parliament. A compromise was reached whereby the Penryn seat only would be transferred, but the House of Lords obstructed the transfer, whereupon Huskisson and his friends voted against the government on the arrangement for East Retford, and offered their resignations. They were accepted by Wellington with unseemly readiness, and Huskisson, Palmerston and the Earl of Dudley thus left the government. Their departure weakened the ministry and the Tory party, in which there now seemed to be no place for even the most moderate reformers. The Liberal Tories were soon to join themselves with the Whigs, reinforcing the progressive element among them and so laying the foundations of the Liberal party which was to be such a force in politics for the century to come.

5 Catholic emancipation
The nightmare of invasion by Catholic powers, urged on by the Pope and supported by Catholic rebels in the British Isles, had haunted the English Protestant

mind since the time of Mary, Queen of Scots, and had been powerfully revived by the policy of King James II. Subordination of the Catholics was therefore an important feature of the Revolution Settlement of 1688, and was defended by Peel and others for that reason, for they were convinced that any weakening of the connection between the state and the Protestant Church of England would endanger the constitution. The only real ground for such fears was now to be found in the condition of Ireland,* for there were no more than 600,000 native English Catholics, whose loyalty was not in question. In Ireland, on the other hand, four-fifths of the population were Catholic, and the country was in a state of almost ceaseless turmoil. There had been a full-scale rebellion in 1798, during the French Revolutionary War, which had been suppressed without great difficulty but with fearful atrocities on both sides. With Ireland's deplorable history in mind, most nineteenth-century Englishmen thought of 'Catholics' as Irish peasants, half savage and wholly untrustworthy, and took little account of the responsibility of English rulers since the time of Cromwell for the desperate condition of the Irish people. While the Catholic question was therefore an Irish one, it is not true that the Irish question was essentially a Catholic one. The disabilities of the Catholics had been partly removed, and those that remained aggravated but did not cause the disorders from which the country was suffering. These arose from its economic backwardness—the lack of industry and low agricultural production. In an overpopulated countryside small peasant farmers could never produce a surplus to raise the standard of living nor a reserve for capital improvements. These conditions were worsened by a rapid increase of population that began in the second half of the eighteenth century. It was not unnatural, however, that the Irish people should blame the English and the Irish Protestants for their misery. Most land was owned by Protestants, and the landlords were often absentees, interested only in screwing out of the tenantry as much rent as possible. The Protestant Church of Ireland was well endowed with land, and

* For an account of this *see* K. H. Randell, *Politics and the People 1835-1850* in this series

collected tithe to support an ample number of clergy ministering to a fraction of the people, while the Irish had to provide for the Roman Catholic Church without assistance. And finally, while Catholics now had the vote, they were barred by law from government service and the House of Commons. 'Catholic emancipation' meant the removal of these disabilities, and was held by its advocates to be the key to all the problems of Ireland. It can now be seen that it was nothing of the kind; there was in fact hardly any improvement in the condition of the country until large and bold agrarian reforms were put in hand towards the end of the nineteenth century. Meanwhile the mass of the Irish people continued in their state of wretchedness and endemic disorder, varied only by periods of famine and relieved only by emigration.

Since the Union had come into effect in 1801, without emancipation, the condition of Ireland had been a standing reproach to British statesmen, none of whom was blind to its seriousness. One emergency measure had followed another; hardly for a year had the country been governed by ordinary legal processes, yet still agitation and violence continued. Why, then, was nothing done? While George III lived there was immovable resistance to any measure giving Catholics political equality with Protestants; his refusal to accept emancipation had caused its exclusion from the Act of Union and Pitt's consequent resignation in 1801. George IV was hardly less inflexible, and gave way only when there was no real alternative. But there was a greater obstacle than the royal conscience and the reluctance of Tories to coerce the sovereign. Their disagreements among themselves were so acute that any attempt to face the issue threatened the disruption of the party and the end of Tory rule. So for fifteen years after 1812 a succession of ministries held to the 'open policy', which was no policy at all. Members of the Cabinet could hold and utter what opinions they pleased, and the government as a whole remained uncommitted. In other words, the problem was put off until it could be put off no longer.

Few of the leading Tories doubted that emancipation must come at some time or other. This was certainly the belief of

Liverpool (though he was personally opposed to it), but the unity of the government was always his first consideration. Wellington's attitude was similar, though with a sufficiently obedient Tory following he might have been ready to meet the Catholics' demands. Even Peel believed that emancipation must come, but he opposed it steadfastly until the last moment. At the root of his hostility may have been the distrust of Catholics developed during his period as Chief Secretary (1812-18), which Halévy describes as his 'loathing for the Irish'. But he was also genuinely convinced that emancipation would endanger not only the connection between Great Britain and Ireland but the fabric ·of the constitution itself. At the opposite pole from Peel was Canning, who showed no concern for human rights, but believed as a matter of expediency that emancipation was inevitable. Yet he accepted the 'open policy' for some years, including the period when he led the Liberal wing of the government, and when he took office as Prime Minister with Whig support still refused to pledge himself to emancipation.

The Whigs being solidly in favour of it, however, a majority for emancipation in the Commons was by no means an impossibility. As early as 1819 a motion of approval failed by only two votes, and in 1821 an emancipation Bill was actually passed in the lower House, but since the Irish Catholic clergy objected to the safeguards included in it, especially a government veto on the appointment of bishops, the House of Lords could hardly be blamed for rejecting it. This was not to be the last occasion of a clash between the Houses on the Catholic question, which, until the question of parliamentary reform arose, was the most prolific cause of conflict between Lords and Commons, as it was of dissension within the Tory party.

From Ireland came an impetus in 1823 in sharp contrast to the uncertain manœuvrings at Westminster, and in the space of two years a first-rate political crisis developed. Daniel O'Connell (1775-1847), an Irish Catholic barrister, who had led the campaign for emancipation since 1808,* had a colourful character and

* For a discussion of his character and achievement *see* K. H. Randell, *Politics and the People 1835-1850* in this series

remarkable oratorical talent. He had killed a man in a duel, and was prevented by arrest from fighting another with Peel in 1820. In 1823 he was one of the founders of the Catholic Association, which began mildly enough as a group of barristers formed to spread propaganda for emancipation. It grew rapidly, however, and with the invention of the Catholic rent—a subscription of a penny a month, usually collected by the parish priests—it gathered large funds and massive numbers. When delegates from the whole country met in Dublin to discuss political questions, the resemblance to an Irish parliament was obvious, and to the government most alarming. So was the prospect of widespread disorder, never far away in Ireland, and now more than likely despite O'Connell's exhortations to constitutional procedure. The Catholic Association was therefore banned by Act of Parliament in 1825—a ban which O'Connell found no difficulty in evading— but the Whigs took the opportunity to urge the removal of Catholic grievances, and Sir Francis Burdett brought in a motion in favour of emancipation which was carried by a majority of seventeen votes. It was followed up by a Bill, with strong safe- guards, including the payment of the Catholic clergy by the state. To these terms O'Connell, now taking a conciliatory line, gave his assent, and the Bill was supported by the Liberal Tory ministers, Canning, Huskisson and Robinson. But Peel was as implacably opposed as ever, and was near to resigning in protest against the policy of his colleagues. After passing in the House of Commons by 248 votes to 227, the Bill met with its expected fate in the upper House, where 130 peers voted for it and 170 against after a menacing intervention by the Duke of York, the King's brother and heir-apparent to the throne, who declared that he would never, as King, give his assent to equality of status for Catholics.

The government had nearly broken up over the issue of eman- cipation, and if the general election which was nearly due had been held immediately there would have been complete con- fusion among the Tories. Canning, however, persuaded the Prime Minister to postpone the election till the following year and the Opposition to let the matter rest meanwhile. Since emancipation had become almost the badge of the Canningites this was an inglorious stance for their leader, but Canning obviously calculated that his prestige in the country, high as it stood, was not sufficient to overcome the hostile forces of the Crown, the House of Lords, the anti-Catholics in his own party, and the 'No Popery' prejudices of the people. So the 'open policy', better described now as a state of deadlock, was continued. Well might Grey ask, in a letter to Brougham, 'It may be convenient to *us*, to have no Catholic question; but is it equally good for the Irish? Have they ever got anything except what has been extorted in the hour of distress? Is it not then *their* interest to keep alive and to inflame a spirit of discontent for that reason?' That it was their interest O'Connell was well aware, and now that he had discovered how to harness the discontent of the Irish peasants in their millions, a new force could be brought into action to break the deadlock.

Before O'Connell again took the initiative, however, the resistance of the anti-Catholics was weakened by an almost incidental change. Ever since the reign of Charles II Protestant Dissenters as well as Roman Catholics had been debarred by the Test and Corporation Acts from holding public office or sitting in Parliament. In fact the laws were inoperative, and every year Parliament passed an Act to indemnify Dissenters who had broken them. In 1827 the Nonconformist bodies made a concerted move to get the statutes repealed. The Whigs had always been friendly to their cause, and now the Tory champions of the Church of England had reason to be grateful for their support in resisting Catholic emancipation. So when Lord John Russell moved the repeal of the Test and Corporation Acts in the House of Commons, the government decided not to oppose it, and it passed easily through both Houses of Parliament. It would now be more difficult indeed to refuse a similar concession to the Roman Catholics.

O'Connell's next step brought the issue suddenly to a head in 1828. Wellington, now Prime Minister in succession to Canning and Goderich, appointed as President of the Board of Trade an Irish M.P., Vesey Fitzgerald. As the law then stood, he had to submit himself for re-election. He was personally in favour of emancipation, and his re-election seemed a foregone conclusion. But he was not unopposed in County Clare. O'Connell himself, though a Catholic, stood against him, and was elected by a large majority. He was declared, not to have been returned to Parliament, but to have gained a majority of the votes. What was the government to do? At the next general election most of the Irish constituencies would follow the example of County Clare, and unless the law was changed Irish representation at Westminster would break down. Not only that, Ireland was in a ferment and civil war was imminent. The law banning the Catholic Association had been passed to operate for three years only; it was now openly re-formed, as were the rival organisations of Orangemen in northern Ireland.

At first it seemed that the government was determined not to yield, especially when Lord Anglesey, who was thought to have shown excessive sympathy with the Catholic cause, was dismissed from the position of Lord Lieutenant and replaced by a reputed anti-Catholic. Yet the King's speech on opening Parliament in February 1829 foretold an emancipation measure, for Wellington had been convinced by the County Clare election that the step was inevitable. It was not really a sudden decision; the long years of the 'open policy' had seen a shift of opinion, reluctant but inescapable. The usual Tory formula for government—control by local authorities, and minor reforms when necessary—would not work in Ireland. The landowners had lost control, and local administration was paralysed. So far from the Roman Catholic clergy being a supporting influence, they had recently become a revolutionary one. Minor reforms had been numerous, from Peel's time onwards: grants of money for public works, the removal of the customs barrier between Great Britain and Ireland, the reform of the magistracy, the establishment of a constabulary, the option to pay tithes in money instead of in kind. As late as 1824 Lord Wellesley when Lord Lieutenant had given a most optimistic report on the beneficial effects of these measures. Yet the state of things in 1829 was such that unless O'Connell and his followers were appeased by emancipation Ireland would be out of control. Wellington's experience told him that 25,000 men—

and no more were available—could not hold down the country, and if Britain should become involved in foreign war the situation would be most perilous.

In the face of this threatening situation debates in Parliament were almost academic, and so pressing was the need for haste that there could be no long haggling over terms. The government's measures were very simple. One Act decreed the end of the Catholic Association—a mere matter of form, since its object had now been achieved. A second repealed all laws which subjected Catholics to civil disabilities, except that a Catholic could not be Lord Lieutenant of Ireland or Lord Chancellor of Ireland or England. A third Act raised the qualification for the vote in the Irish counties from forty shillings to ten pounds. The last was designed to keep out of Parliament representatives, who would now be Catholics, of the mass of the Irish peasantry. Of the many safeguards that had been long under discussion this was the only one enacted; Wellington and Peel dropped the rest to hasten the passage of the Bills, which occupied little more than two months. They disregarded both their earlier anxieties and the state of opinion in the country, where a majority of the people, as the general election of 1826 had made fairly clear, was opposed to emancipation.

In Parliament, on the other hand, the balance of debate was heavily in its favour. The argument that told was not equality of human rights; this served the Whigs as a debating point, but was somewhat spoiled by their accepting the disfranchisement of so many of the Irish people. The traditional arguments against emancipation were easily demolished. The sanctity of the Revolution Settlement could not be invoked because the grant of equal rights to Nonconformists had already breached it. The dangers from Roman Catholic Powers abroad had faded into insignificance; the French and Spanish governments were themselves threatened by popular movements, against which the Tories wanted the British government to help them. Least of all could the Papacy be described as a menace. The best argument against emancipation was that it would not solve the problems of

Ireland—a prophecy that was only too true, but it weighed little against the urgent realities of the situation.

These were the main theme of a masterly four-hour speech by Peel which would have compelled the highest admiration had not the House remembered how often and how forcefully he had argued the opposite case. If he was right now in advocating emancipation he could be blamed for persisting so long in opposing it. If he had been right before he could plead no sufficient reason for changing his mind. Prof. Gash, in *Mr. Secretary Peel*, argues in his defence that 'politics is not merely an exercise in the art of prevision'. His belief in the importance of the tie between the state and the Church of England was genuine. So were his distrust of the Irish and his fear that concessions would only lead to further demands and eventually to separation. But he saw by 1825 that the situation had changed: the English ruling class had lost the will and the ability to maintain their hold on Ireland, where government was breaking down. It was certainly Peel's hope that some other leader—Canning, until his death—would take the necessary step. Then came the County Clare election and the urgent need for a solution, and it was Peel himself who had to introduce the emancipation measures in the House of Commons —or resign. If he had resigned the government would have fallen, the Whigs would have come in, and emancipation would have been granted—if Ireland had not first dissolved into revolution and civil war. It is hard to assert that in these circumstances he should have resigned, but he never overcame the distrust and bitterness which many Tories felt, and he himself became more withdrawn and harsh and prone to self-justification.

The emancipation Bill passed the Commons by 320 votes to 142, the Whigs voting with the government, and the 'anti-Catholic' (or Ultra-) Tories against it. In the Lords there was a majority of only two votes, 111 to 109, but several bishops voted for it. George IV delayed his assent till the very last moment, and then yielded only to avoid the greater evil of the Duke's resignation and the advent of the Whigs. The Tory party seemed to be in ruins; the Liberals were already estranged from the rest, and now there was an open rift between the supporters and opponents of emancipation. The latter became unexpected recruits to the cause of parliamentary reform, claiming with some reason that the greater part of the nation was on their side, and that only a Parliament which failed to represent the people could have voted for emancipation. Such enthusiasm for democracy was dangerous for Tories, and did not last very long. More important was the direct encouragement given to the movement for parliamentary reform by O'Connell's example of successful agitation; the Birmingham Political Union was soon to copy deliberately the methods of the Catholic Association.

Halévy describes the achievement of Catholic emancipation as 'a victory for a Liberal aristocracy and middle class over the Conservative prejudice of the nation'. But in fact this battle was never joined: the anti-Catholic prejudice of the people was circumvented rather than overcome, though if it had been raised to a higher pitch this might not have been possible. G. I. T. Machin, in *The Catholic Question in English Politics, 1820-1830*, concludes that anti-Catholic feeling, though not dead, lay dormant during this crisis. Moreover, to claim that the aristocracy and the middle class, divided as they were, showed themselves liberal is to do them too much honour. Emancipation was granted for reasons of expediency, and the victor was Daniel O'Connell, as leader of a people oppressed by centuries of English rule. It would take more than emancipation to appease them.

Chapter V

The Reform of Parliament

1 The Whigs come to power The last months of Wellington's ministry gave few signs of the dramatic change in political fortunes which was to end the era of the Tories by bringing in the Whigs and a reform of the parliamentary system. Far from relentlessly attacking the Duke, now deserted by many of the Tories, the Whigs deliberately made things easy for him, since they preferred him to the most likely alternative—a government of the Ultra-Tories—and there was even talk of their joining him in a coalition. Nor was it obvious that a struggle for parliamentary reform was imminent. The agitation in the country had died down; there was greater concern over economic than political questions: demand for many types of goods was slack, farm prices, except for wheat, were falling, and there was much distress in both town and country.

Nor did the general election in July 1830, necessitated by the death of George IV and the accession of his brother, the Duke of Clarence, as William IV, immediately transform the situation. As usual most of the seats were uncontested, and the voters who went to the polls were confused by the various opposition groups— Ultras, Canningites, Whigs and Radicals. In the more open constituencies, for example in the county of Yorkshire, where Brougham had a triumphant success, there was indeed no doubt about the public's dissatisfaction with the government. But the Opposition could not claim more than a net gain of thirty seats, and Wellington seemed prepared to carry on. He needed, however, a wider base of support. His first attempt to gain it, by a reconciliation with Huskisson on the occasion of the opening of the Liverpool-Manchester Railway, was brought to nought by Huskisson's fatal accident. Wellington next approached Palmerston, but he and his Canningite friends refused to co-operate unless the ministry and its policy were completely reconstructed. The Whigs now took up a much more hostile attitude, in response to which the Duke made his famous speech in the House of Lords proclaiming the perfection of the British constitution and his opposition to any change whatever in the electoral system. It is possible that he hoped in this way to bring back the Ultras to his side, but if so he failed, while virtually driving Palmerston and the other Canningites out of the Tory party. In November, on a motion for a select committee on the new King's civil list, the government was defeated in the Commons by a combination of the Whigs, the Canningites, the Ultras (seeking revenge for Catholic emancipation) and most of the country members. Wellington resigned and advised the King to send for Lord Grey (1764-1845), which he did without hesitation. It was the first time since 1804 that a ministry had been forced to resign by an adverse majority in the House of Commons, and the result was the first complete change of ministers since 1807.

The nation's temperature had risen swiftly since the first half of the year, and not only because of the political crisis and Wellington's infuriating speech. While the general election was in progress news had come of the revolution in France and the flight of King Charles X, who had attempted to set aside the constitution and establish arbitrary rule with the help of the ultra-Conservatives. In England there were Radical demonstrations to show solidarity with the French liberals, and in the later stages of the election parliamentary reform, instead of retrenchment and the abolition of slavery, became the chief rallying-cry. Social distress in many parts of the country provided the fuel for agitation; for a few days London mobs threatened to get out of hand, while agrarian riots spread rapidly through the counties nearest the metropolis. The situation was dangerous, but if the Whigs could ride the storm they would emerge triumphant. By offering the country a reform of Parliament they could attract support from all classes, while at Westminster their party, so long moribund, would draw new life from the campaign. The adhesion of the Liberal Tories would reinforce its talent and strengthen its progressive tendencies, and the Radicals would give firm support. Both these groups were represented in Grey's Cabinet, which he took only four days to complete—the Liberal Tories by Palmerston as Foreign Secretary, Melbourne as Home Secretary and Goderich as Secretary for War and Colonies, the Radicals by Durham, Lord Privy Seal, and Brougham, who to his great regret left the Commons, the scene of his many debating triumphs, to become Lord Chancellor. The ministry was the most aristocratic of the century; only four of its members were not in the House of Lords, and of those Althorp was heir to an earldom, Palmerston held an Irish peerage, and Lord John Russell was the third son of the Duke of Bedford. Such a ministry was an assurance to the propertied classes that reform did not mean revolution.

The assurance was grimly underlined by the way the ministry dealt with the agrarian disturbances which had broken out in August, before Wellington's resignation. This last English agrarian revolt seems to have been in general a spontaneous outbreak, for 'Captain Swing', who was spoken of as the leader, was an entirely mythical figure. It is unlikely that French Jacobin agents had a hand in it, as Wellington supposed, though the news from France caused some excitement, while a speaking tour by Cobbett through the southern counties may have helped to stir up trouble. There was, however, plentiful cause for unrest in the condition of the country labourers. The poor harvests of 1829 and 1830 had raised the price of bread, and there was much unemployment. Some authorities tried to reduce the rate of poor relief, which in total made up fifteen per cent of the income of rural labourers. There was most disturbance where casual labour was widely employed, and in the larger villages where skilled craftsmen could provide leadership. The main objectives of the rioters were regular employment and higher wages (they often asked for 2s 6d a day), and their main activity was breaking up threshing machines, which were hated not only as almost the only power-driven machines on the farms, but because they deprived men of work in the winter months when their needs were greatest and there was no alternative way of earning money.

So confident were the rioters of the justice of their complaints that they expected public support. They were not entirely disappointed, for the magistrates of Norfolk issued a proclamation urging farmers to destroy their machines and raise wages to 10s a week. Elsewhere farmers were known to join the labourers in petitions for the lowering of taxes and tithes, which they were very willing to blame as the real causes of rural hardships. 'Captain Swing' destroyed a great deal of machinery and extorted 'gifts' of money, but there was not much rick-burning and no one was killed—not even an overseer of the poor. This moderation might have evoked a more merciful response from the government, but the ministers feared that disorder would spread to the towns and, in view of the general state of the country, might escalate into revolution. Melbourne (1779-1848), the Home Secretary, was convinced that only with the utmost firmness could order be preserved while a reform of Parliament was going through. With a reputation for idleness and frivolity, he now astonished everyone by the vigour of his repressive measures; his exhortations to the magistrates outdid those of Sidmouth. Robbery and rioting were of course still capital offences, and 252 men were sentenced to death, though only nineteen were actually executed. Nearly five hundred were transported to Australia, most having committed no previous offence; the pardons granted later did not bring them back to England. In three months these relentless measures fully restored order.

To some degree the riots achieved their purpose: the use of threshing machines was halted for a time, and on some farms wages were raised, temporarily at least. But in general rural workers remained in their degraded and demoralised state until at last agricultural depression passed away in the 1850s. Professors Hobsbawm and Rudé, in *Captain Swing* (1969), are inclined to accept Cobbett's opinion that the riots played a major part in bringing about parliamentary reform, though they accept that there was no contact between the rioters and urban Radicals. They go on to suggest that it may have influenced the reform legislation of 1832-35: 'It would be surprising if a movement so widespread, and which frightened the government so much—for however brief a spell—had been without influence on reform legislation.' Before this suggestion is fully accepted it must be remembered that governments had been frightened in 1816-19 without producing reforms, and in the 1820s had produced reforms without being frightened; also that the riots of 1830 were most effectively, if cruelly, suppressed. This is not to deny, however, the effect of opinion in the country generally on the fortunes of the proposals for the reform of Parliament first launched in the spring of 1831.

2 The Reform Bills The Whig proposals for the reform of Parliament were prepared in detail by a committee of four members of the Cabinet (Lord John Russell (1792-1878) and Lord Brougham (1778-1868) were the prime movers), were approved by the Cabinet, accepted with surprising promptitude by the King, and put forward in the House of Commons by Lord John Russell on 1 March 1831. The first challenge from the Tories came on the second reading of the Bill, which passed, amid scenes of great excitement, by one vote—302 to 301. The government was soon defeated, however, when the Bill was considered in detail, on a clause which would reduce the number of English seats in order to increase the Scottish and Irish representation. The government refused to accept the defeat, and secured from the King the dissolution of Parliament so that another election might be held. Its purpose was obviously to return a House which would pass a Reform Bill, and the result left no doubt of the country's wishes: the government, which had been in a minority, now had a majority in the Commons of 140.

A second Reform Bill was introduced in the new parliament, and after Tory amendments to add tenants to the county franchise—and so increase landlord influence—had been accepted by the government, it passed the House of Commons by a large majority. The Tories in the House of Lords were determined to resist, and the Bill was rejected by the alarmingly large majority of 41. Grey then declared that he would persist in seeking a reform 'as effective' as the one just rejected, and Parliament was prorogued for a month, during which agitation in the country was extreme.

When Parliament reassembled, Lord John Russell presented a third Reform Bill which showed no important difference from the second except in increasing the number of seats so that England and Wales should have undiminished representation. This Bill also passed the Commons by a large majority, though the Tories, led by Peel, voted solidly against it. The most critical moment had now arrived. Would the Tory peers reject a reform Bill for the second time? This proved not to be their intention, but, judging the country to be in a calmer mood in the early months of 1832, and discerning signs, as they thought, that the government's resolution was weakening, they planned to use their majority to take over the Bill and force upon the government their own amendments to it. When, however, they carried the first of these, which would have deferred the vital first clause of the Bill disfranchising the rotten boroughs, Grey refused to accept the amendment, and immediately asked the King to create enough peers to overcome the Tory opposition. When the King refused, Grey resigned. The King then invited Wellington to form a ministry, with the remarkable request that it should put through a Bill on the same lines as the Whig one. Still more remarkable was the Duke's acceptance of the task, presumably out of a sense of duty, but he failed to persuade his Tory colleagues, notably Peel, to emulate his flexibility, and so had to report failure to the King. William IV had now no choice but to recall the Whigs, and to promise Grey in writing that he would create the necessary number of peers to overcome any opposition to the Bill. Only under this threat did Wellington give an undertaking to let the Bill through, which he did by abstaining from voting, being followed by all but twenty-seven Tory peers. In June 1832 the Bill became law.

What forces were brought into play to win the stubborn and dramatic struggle for reform? In particular, how were the constitutional proceedings affected by popular movements outside Parliament? It is impossible, in the first place, to ignore the effect

of economic dislocation and social distress, though it was anything but a novel factor. It was not only the bad harvests of 1829
and 1830 and the consequently high price of bread, but depression in a number of industries which made 1830, like 1817, 1819
and 1826, a year of exceptional suffering and unrest. Hence the
demand during the election of 1830 for retrenchment and lower
taxes, a demand which the first Whig budget did nothing to
satisfy. By 1831 all the manufacturing districts were affected by
the depression, and discontent was general and intense. It is
remarkable that in the towns it still took the form almost solely
of a campaign for parliamentary reform. The credit may belong in
large measure to the spread of knowledge and reasoned discussion since 1815 by the Radical organisations and the rapidly
expanding newspapers. In 1830-31 there was a new spate of unstamped Radical journals, of which Henry Hetherington's *Poor
Man's Guardian* was the most important, while Cobbett, who had
been unusually quiet for some time, produced a new burst of
propagandist activity, and when put on trial for sedition in
November, 1830, was triumphantly acquitted. News from France,
where the revolution promised a generous grant of political
rights, was eagerly read in England, and was partly responsible
for the succession of meetings and demonstrations that filled the
early months of 1831. The same year saw the formation in
London of the National Union of the Working Classes, which
demanded manhood suffrage and the ballot.

Agitation was not confined, however, to the working classes. In
the early months of 1830 a number of county meetings were held
in which the gentry demanded better representation for the
counties as against the boroughs. In the general atmosphere of
expectation the Political Unions flourished anew, led by the
Union in Birmingham founded by Thomas Attwood, banker and
professed Tory, whose first enthusiasm was currency reform, but
who, when that seemed hopeless, turned to electoral reform
instead. The Unions pressed their claims through petitions to
Parliament; it was an important feature of the Reform crisis that
the relations between the House of Commons and the people were
closer than ever before, thanks to the detailed reporting in the

Press of debates and divisions, and to a flood of popular petitions, each of which could be the subject of a debate—until the Whigs restricted the practice in 1831. At first the Political Unions had a strongly middle-class character, but most of them soon admitted working-class members and canvassed strongly Radical programmes. This was symbolic of a change which had taken place generally since the earlier agitations for parliamentary reform. The propertied classes, either because they were less afraid of the workers, or because they thought them more dangerous while denied political rights, were willing, despite periodic alarms, to take the lower orders into partnership in the struggle for reform.

The general election of 1831, following the defeat of the government on the first Reform Bill, gave unmistakable evidence of the widespread demand for reform. It is true that influences of the customary kind were at work—the boroughs controlled by the Treasury now of course returned Whigs instead of Tories, and the Scottish members were as usual amenable to the government's bidding—but the government's majority of 140 left no room for doubt that the country was determined to have the electoral system changed. The storm provoked by the peers' rejection of the second Bill was therefore predictable. The majorities in the hereditary and the elected House were now deadlocked. If the peers persisted, the deadlock could be broken constitutionally only by the King, who so far was unwilling to create new peers; it could be broken unconstitutionally by the populace, who might be provoked into revolution. This was plainly threatened in the last months of 1831. There was an outbreak of arson in the southern counties; in Nottingham the Castle, which belonged to the Duke of Newcastle, and in Bristol the Bishop's Palace were burned down—only two bishops had voted for the Bill. It was at this time that the Union of the Working Classes was formed, and the government was sufficiently alarmed to consult Wellington about military precautions in the capital.

In 'the days of May', 1832, when Grey resigned and Wellington tried to form a ministry, the outburst was more organised, and for that reason more threatening. There were plans for an armed rising, to begin in Birmingham the moment the Duke took office, and the Radicals claimed there were retired officers available to lead it. Measures of another kind were in hand which indicate reliance on general support from the middle class. The combined Political Unions, with Place's tailor's shop as headquarters, were planning a tax strike and a take-over of local government throughout the country. But the immediate step was to be an organised run on the banks, which would paralyse all business, and for which Place coined the slogan that suddenly appeared on posters everywhere: 'To stop the Duke, go for gold.' He later claimed, on the evidence of a Cabinet minister, that Wellington's surrender and the King's recall of Grey were due to a message sent to Grey by the directors of the Bank of England, and passed on by him to Wellington, warning that all the banks would be forced to close in a few days if there was a run on gold.

It is difficult to measure the effect of popular agitation on the proceedings at Westminster. The state of the country was not mentioned by either Tories or Whigs during exchanges in Parliament. The Whigs did not like the accusation that they were in league with unconstitutional forces to defeat an opposition to their Bills which was maintained by constitutional means, though the charge was true. Information was passed to Place and others by such Radical ministers as Lord Durham, while Place on his side carefully fed to Melbourne, the Home Secretary, news of the explosive temper of the people. After the crisis Grey formally thanked Attwood for his help. Whether Grey stressed the dangers of the situation to the King in order to extract his promise to create peers is not known. But it is difficult to believe that without the threat of revolution, substantiated as it was by many incidents of violence, Grey would have stuck to his uncongenial task, that the Cabinet would have refused any major modification of their Bill, or that the King would have agreed to swamp the House of Lords with new Whig peers.

The whole strategy of the Whigs had been to fortify the elements of order in the nation, which they identified as the propertied classes, and which in fact they called 'the people'. Brougham said in 1831, 'By the People, I mean the middle classes, the wealth and intelligence of the country, the glory of the British name.' Grey spoke of the middle class as 'the real and efficient mass of public opinion, without whom the power of the gentry is nothing'. The Whigs were as much afraid of the masses as the Tories were, but believed that the middle class must be won over to the side of the aristocracy. With this reinforcement of half a million solid citizens property would be secure. If on the other hand the middle class were denied its political rights, it would give leaders to the working class in a struggle which might end in the overthrow of property and a democracy of the masses.

The politics of the Tories also hinged on property. They believed its protection to be the main function of the constitution, and therefore saw the Reform Bills as an unprecedented and intolerable attack on vested rights. 'A shake will be given to the property of every individual in the country', Wellington said. Nor would they resign themselves to sharing power with the middle class; they viewed with horror the prospect of the House of Commons emptied of gentlemen and filled with lawyers, tradesmen, and demagogues. Peel took a gloomy view of the future consequences of reform which proved to be fully justified: the lower House would come to dominate the upper, thus upsetting the balance of the constitution; there would be a conflict between the landed and industrial interests in which the latter would prevail; and, whereas the Whigs believed their generous measure of reform would be final, Peel said, 'I was unwilling to open a door which I saw no prospect of being able to close.' The door remained open to admit the representation not only of every form of property, but ultimately of the whole adult population. The Whigs, seeking to give a broader interpretation to the eighteenth century themes of property and interest, in fact were undermining them.

3 The significance of the Reform Act The terms of the Reform Act of 1832 differed little from those of the first Bill introduced by Lord John Russell. Fifty-six boroughs with populations under 2000 lost both their members, and thirty others with fewer than 4000 people lost one. The representation of the counties was increased by no fewer than sixty-one members, a handsome present to the landed interest. The counties were still under-represented compared with the boroughs, but the injustice was more apparent than real, for many borough boundaries were extended to include a sufficient population to qualify for a member, thus producing a constituency which was more rural than urban. Twenty-two new boroughs—populous towns and four districts of London—were to have two members each, and twenty were to have one. In the allocation of seats to boroughs, numerical equality received less attention than the representation of particular interests, e.g., woollen manufacture in Frome and shipbuilding in Whitby. The south of England was still too heavily represented, and the new industrial cities of the north left with too few members, but the new distribution of seats partially reflected the changed distribution of the population.

Boroughs and counties were each to have a uniform franchise. In the boroughs this was simply the occupation of a house, shop, warehouse, etc., of annual value not less than £10. In London, where houses were expensive, this was not far off a household franchise, but in many towns most of the working-class people and the lower middle class would be excluded. About half the properties that qualified were worth £20 per annum or more, so that on average the borough electorate would be fairly prosperous. Most of the classes qualified in the old 'popular' boroughs would now lose the franchise, of course; not until 1918 would the adult males of Preston fully recover their rights. It was provided, however, that no one possessed of the franchise in 1832 should lose it during his lifetime, and this told in favour of the poorer voters. In the counties voting rights were more complicated. To the forty-shilling freeholders were added copyholders whose land was worth at least £10 a year, holders of leases of the same value if of sixty years' duration, and of leases for twenty years of £50 annual value, and, finally, tenants of any kind who paid £50 a year in rent. This last class had been added as the result of a Tory amendment to the Bill designed to increase landlord influence; the amendment had been supported by the Radicals and accepted by the government.

There were in fact three Reform Acts, one for each of the three kingdoms. Scotland was the scene of the biggest change, the electorate being increased from a few thousand to 65,000, but the number who qualified in the counties by ownership or a life lease of land worth £10 a year was very small, and the continued domination of landlords was inevitable. In Ireland the changes now made were few because of those already decided in 1800 or 1829. The £10 qualification in the boroughs left half of them with fewer than 300 voters, so that influence and corruption continued to flourish there, while the counties were under-represented. Ireland gained the most seats by the redistribution, but of course had the largest proportion of voteless people. Altogether Wales, Scotland and Ireland increased their representation at the expense of England. The new electorate did not reach the million foretold by Lord John Russell. The number who registered in 1832 was 813,000, compared with under 500,000 before the Act. For the United Kingdom as a whole this meant one in seven of adult males—for England and Wales one in five, for Scotland one in eight, for Ireland one in twenty.

These measures were satisfactory, as they were intended to be, to the more prosperous of the middle class, but worse than disappointing to the working-class Radicals, who felt they had been betrayed; without pressure from the working class the middle class might not have got the vote, but the working class was left outside the 'political nation'. Moreover the ballot, for years an important feature of Radical demands and now enjoyed by the voters of France, was withheld, primarily through Grey's implacable opposition. So was a shortening of the life of a parliament, which remained seven years. On the other hand the Whigs could claim that they had removed the main anomalies of the electoral system—the great expense of elections, the choice of M.P.s by close corporations, and, worst of all, the nomination of members by private individuals—and that these changes had involved an attack on property without precedent.

How would the Reform Act work out in the generation that was to elapse before the next reform of Parliament? The more closely the parliamentary scene and the electoral processes are examined (as they have been, for example, by Professor Norman Gash in *Politics in the Age of Peel*), the less dramatic seems the contrast between the unreformed and the new systems. In the first place the membership of the House of Commons was little changed in character. The property qualification remained, while the expense of elections and the necessary sacrifice by an M.P. of remunerative employment limited membership to men of independent means. Besides, the new electors often seemed to prefer gentry to candidates of their own kind. In the constituencies the old evils persisted until in 1872 the Ballot Act provided an effective remedy. Half the English boroughs had fewer than a thousand voters, so bribery was still widely practised; in many boroughs the price of a vote was generally known. Candidates and voters suffered violence before and during elections, though this was seldom on a large scale except in times of economic distress. It was still considered quite proper for a tenant to be directed by his landlord in the use of his vote, while in many boroughs ties of family or interest continued to dictate the choice of members. Professor Gash estimates that some sixty M.P.s in England and Wales owed their seats to the influence of great landowners, and that forty peers were still able to nominate a member of the Commons, though now not more than one each. There continued to be a very large proportion of uncontested elections, averaging nearly a half in the five elections that followed the Reform Act. Often a contest was avoided by some arrangement made in advance on the basis of local and personal interests, so that party discipline was considerably weakened.

Professor Gash makes the interesting point that the absence of a ballot often made for a better expression of the interests of a constituency than secrecy would have allowed. Voters were subject to pressure, and though the pressure was sometimes of an unpleasant kind it nevertheless compelled attention to the wishes of the voteless members of the community. Wherever ordinary social and economic relationships involved dependence, influence could be brought to bear: the shopkeeper, for example, would be under pressure to vote as his customers wished. There must have been many boroughs where elections were now decided not by the instructions of a landlord but by the importunity of the people in general.

The most definite result of the wider borough franchise and the redistribution of seats was the reduction of government influence. The Treasury borough, where votes were safely bought with government funds, was a thing of the past, and there were now very few constituencies where the votes of government employees could be decisive. In the government service, too, promotion was now less likely to depend on voting allegiance than on merit. In one important respect the new electoral system made it more difficult for the Prime Minister to shuffle his Cabinet, for on appointment to an office a minister had to seek re-election, and there were now no boroughs at the government's disposal where his return would be certain.

Political patronage in general, which in the eighteenth century had been the cement of the constitution, was now much less important, though it would not disappear until new and impartial means were evolved for filling posts in government service. Sinecures had been effectively abolished, but a large number of government appointments were made through the Patronage Secretary at the Treasury, who was also the chief Whip. Naturally the government's favours were distributed in such a way as to reward or create support. But nearly all the posts at the Treasury's disposal were minor ones and poorly paid. Moreover the governments of this period were very sensitive to accusations that they were purchasing support by scattering largesse. Due rewards for the faithful were a different matter, and no doubt strengthened party ties, but it is doubtful whether the results in electoral votes or in support in the House of Commons were worth the vast amount of correspondence and fuss involved, as may be shown by the inability of the Whigs, despite their control of patronage after 1830, to prevent the loss of their majority and their eventual defeat in 1841. The influence of patronage would in time be completely replaced by the influence of party, and to this the Reform Act gave a stimulus by requiring the registration of voters. In order to organise the registration of their supporters the parties began to build up permanent clubs both in the constituencies and in London (where the Tory Carlton Club and the Whig Reform Club were founded in the 1830s) which were to have an increasing influence on the shaping of policy and the conduct of the politicians in Parliament.

This development, however, was slow, and was still incomplete when the second Reform Act was passed in 1867. Meanwhile with neither patronage nor party dominant in the House of Commons, the private member enjoyed greater importance; at no other time were his speeches likely to be so influential inside Parliament or so well reported in the Press, where long reports of debates were read with interest by the new middle-class electorate. At the same time the House of Commons had won a larger place in the constitution. While a large and sudden creation of peers was regarded as a violent measure to be employed only as a very last resort, once the threat had been used the House of Lords could never again be regarded as equal in power to the lower House. Similarly the crisis of 1832 had gone far to establish the doctrine that the sovereign must accept the advice of his ministers, and that the making of policy therefore rested in their hands.

We may admire the statesmanship of Grey and his colleagues in accurately judging the measure of reform that the country would accept and Parliament could be persuaded to concede, and their determination and courage in so handling the crisis as to produce reform without revolution. But if we speak of 'the Great Reform Act' it is less because of its intrinsic significance than because of the drama of the struggle to obtain it, less because of its direct than its indirect effects on the constitution in reducing the stature of both monarchy and House of Lords, less because of its immediate than its more remote political consequences in engendering conflict between the two Houses and opening the way to more democratic change.

Chapter VI

Further Reforms

1 The reform of the municipal corporations and the courts
Prospects for reform seemed bright after the general election
held under the new law in December 1832. In the new House of
Commons there were 320 of Grey's supporters and only 120
Tories. The latter, led by Peel, were now learning from him to
adopt the name and outlook of Conservatives rather than Tories,
that is, to accept the fact of parliamentary reform and not to
obstruct necessary and moderate changes. The Tories in the
upper House might find this attitude uncongenial, but they would
not readily repeat the challenge they had offered over the Reform
Bills. In this situation legislation of a new kind was clearly possible, but the extent and character of the reforms to come were by
no means determined. If there had been a distinctively middle-
class party the position would have been different, but the Whigs
were still led mainly by aristocrats, and the fifty Radicals, however energetic a tail, could not wag the Whig dog. The limited
possibilities of action through Parliament were to be shown up
before the decade ended by the launching of the two greatest
extra-parliamentary movements of the century—Chartism and
the Anti-Corn Law League.*

The cause of reform, however, had one great asset, for Utilitarian doctrine had provided a set of principles, and the Whig
government was ready to apply them. Bentham's passion for

* See K. H. Randell, *Politics and the People 1835-1850* in this series

scientific accuracy also indicated the procedure to be followed: the ascertainment of facts by a commission of inquiry, the framing of legislation on the basis of its report, and the drafting of regulations to be applied by a central administrative authority. The procedure soon revealed a contradiction that was inherent in Utilitarian doctrine: the activity required of the state to ensure the greatest happiness of the greatest number made large inroads on the liberty of the individual, though according to the 'pleasure-pain' principle he was the only judge of what was good for him.* The paradox was bound to emerge as soon as the state began to deal positively with social problems, as it now proceeded to do.

A necessary preliminary to any such activity was a reform of local government, which was accomplished in some measure by the Municipal Corporations Act (1835), following the report of a commission of inquiry set up in 1833. Its secretary was Joseph Parkes, a Birmingham business man and a Radical, who had been extremely active in the campaign for parliamentary reform, and the spirit of the inquiry is reflected in Parkes's greeting for the Act which resulted—'poison for the Tories'. The commission gave prominence to all the worst practices it discovered, and the result was a picture of nepotism, political partisanship, neglect of duties and misappropriation of funds. All of these were possible under the prevailing arrangements, for borough corporations were either self-perpetuating by co-optation, or elected by the freemen, who might be non-resident. Many were filled with the dependents of local landowners, and were likely to be Tory strongholds. The members of the corporation were not responsible to the inhabitants of the borough, and might use their powers and their funds to the advantage of their party or of themselves, especially as a large part of their business was the management of charitable trusts. Their affairs were conducted in secret—there were boroughs where not even the bye-laws were published—and the law was sometimes shockingly administered by magistrates and juries selected without regard to their impartiality or fitness. So it had come about that the important functions of local

* *See* p. 30 above

government, such as street-lighting and paving, drainage and police, were dealt with in many towns by improvement commissions established by private Act of Parliament. The strictures of Parkes and his colleagues were certainly exaggerated, but they contained enough truth to justify a sweeping reform.

By the terms of the Whig Bill the corporations were to be replaced, except in a number of boroughs that lost their status altogether, by a uniform system of councils elected by all householders, resident for three years, who paid the poor rate. This measure was too sweeping to please the Tory peers, whose amendments were perhaps intended to wreck it. However, Peel and Russell arranged a compromise which was accepted by both Houses, and the main features of the resulting Act have lasted until the present time. To the councillors, elected for three years with one-third changing each year, were added aldermen—one-third of the number of councillors and chosen by them—who served for six years. The Act applied only to old boroughs, so that Birmingham and Manchester, for example, were still left without a proper administration, but towns could obtain borough status by petition. The new councils took over existing borough revenues, and were given power to levy rates if necessary, but they lost the right to administer religious trusts, which had led to many abuses. Their primary duties were now to be the supervision, through watch committees, of new police forces, and the provision of street lighting—both intended to improve the maintenance of order—though where there were improvement commissions they were allowed to continue. The borough councils could pass bye-laws for the suppression of nuisances—a very negative safeguard of public health—but otherwise their competence was narrowly limited until fresh tasks were seen to be socially necessary. A similar Act for Scotland was more liberal in the number of boroughs included, but less so in restricting the vote to those who had the parliamentary franchise—the ten-pound householders. The same qualification was adopted in the Irish Act, but there it excluded the majority of householders, and the number of recognised boroughs in any case was very small.

Halévy describes the Municipal Corporations Act as bringing

about 'a social revolution' and establishing in England 'islands of representative democracy'. It is true that a great many Tory oligarchies had been extinguished, and that in the boroughs there was a closer approach to manhood suffrage and annual elections than had been achieved by parliamentary reform, though in some boroughs, because of the residence requirement, the qualified voters were fewer than the holders of the parliamentary franchise. The councils, once established, could be invested by Parliament with further powers, but this development proceeded slowly, and Joseph Parkes was too optimistic when he described the new councils as 'the steam engine for the Mill built by Parliamentary Reform'. The shopkeepers who now dominated many of the towns showed more concern for economy than for improvement. In Birmingham, where the Street Commissioners had been particularly energetic, the city declined into squalor when they handed over their powers to the new council. One verdict is that where petty graft had been prevelant the Act did little more than change the practitioners. As to this change, however, there is no doubt; the middle-class business men took over borough government from the clients of the landowning class, which meant in most cases that Whigs took over from Tories, and that Dissenters, usually excluded hitherto, became prominent in local affairs. The change was the more important because from this time magistrates were usually selected on the recommendation of the councils. A much greater shift of power would of course have resulted from a similar democratisation of government in the rural areas, but this was more than any ministry would attempt until another half-century of squirearchy had passed.

Henry Brougham was appointed by Grey to be Lord Chancellor in 1830 partly at least because he had proved so difficult to control in the House of Commons. Easily the most brilliant figure among the Whig leaders, he had all the talents required for high office—an immense capacity for work, a powerful intellect, and formidable skill in debate—but these were unfortunately spoiled by his instability of character, disloyalty to his colleagues, and behaviour so unpredictable that people sometimes doubted his sanity.

Four years on the Woolsack enabled him to display his talents to the fullest advantage until his unreasonable conduct caused Melbourne to drop him from the Cabinet. They were four years of intense activity during which he implemented a great many of the ideas on legal reform which he had laid before the House of Commons from the Opposition benches in a great speech in 1828.

Peel had left comparatively little to be done in the field of criminal law, but a further number of crimes was removed from the list of capital offences, and Peel's improvements in the prison system, with others now added, were implemented more effectively by the appointment for the first time of inspectors of prisons. Brougham secured many reforms in legal procedure, which were facilitated by the payment of salaries instead of fees to a number of legal officials. The vast arrears of cases in the Court of Chancery were reduced, and its procedure rationalised. The Central Criminal Court and the Bankruptcy Court were instituted in London, and the Judicial Committee of the Privy Council was established to hear appeals from ecclesiastical and colonial courts. A measure to compile a land register aroused too many fears of official inquisitiveness and failed to pass the House of Commons, and another to introduce a new system of local courts to pass the House of Lords, but Brougham could show an impressive record of legal reform, all of it drawn originally from Bentham's storehouse of Utilitarian ideas.

2 The new Poor Law Notable as the reform of the courts was, the greatest triumph of Benthamism was the new Poor Law, which swept away a system established since the time of Elizabeth I, and was itself to last in some respects until the twentieth century. The preliminary investigation, the psychological and moral principles of the new system and the centralised machinery for its operation were all designed on a Utilitarian pattern of the purest kind. No external pressures helped to shape the product; the Poor Law Amendment Act of 1834 was an official measure inspired entirely by the 'philosophic Radicals' and thrust on the country with a self-assurance and a disregard of vested interests that were in equal measure characteristic.

Lord Grey's government, alarmed by the widespread agrarian outbreak of 1830 and by the continuing high cost of poor relief, soon decided on a searching inquiry into its administration. The Elizabethan law of 1601 had decreed that the able-bodied poor should be 'set on work', that the old and infirm should be provided with the necessities of life or the money to buy them, and that the unit of administration should be the parish, in which a special rate should be levied to cover the cost. Overseers of the poor levied the rate and supervised relief under the control of the J.P.s of the county. By the terms of Gilbert's Act of 1782 parishes could combine into unions for the better execution of these duties, particularly the building and management of a workhouse, but most did not.

The system had come under exceptional strain during and since the wars because of bad harvests, depressed agriculture and other causes of distress. In 1795, one of the worst years of the period, the J.P.s of Berkshire, meeting in the village of Speenhamland, reached a decision that was not entirely novel but had never before been widely adopted. They resolved to relieve the acute distress of the people by making allowances of money to all poor families calculated according to the number of children and the current price of bread, and they would when necessary make up the wages of an employed man according to the same scale. The Speenhamland system, usually known at the time as the 'allowance system', spread through about half the counties of England, but it was seldom applied in large towns. At the same time, because of the scale of distress, only a very small proportion of the poor was taken into the poorhouses, and still fewer were given work to do there. Nearly all the overseers' funds were spent on 'out-relief', though there was as a rule an attempt to operate a 'roundsman' system, whereby ratepayers had paupers to work for them in return for their contributions to the poor-rate.

It was claimed that the allowance system saved the country from a revolt of a starving population. Nevertheless it had come to be regarded by the ruling classes as an unmitigated evil. The most obvious objection to it was its cost. The peak figure of nearly £8 million in 1818 quoted by the Commissioners was never reached again, but in 1830-31 the year's expenditure was close on £7 million, some £3 million of which was disbursed to agricultural labourers in the southern half of the country. Payment of allowances for children, legitimate or illegitimate, was held to encourage not only reckless breeding by the poor but immorality. Wages were depressed because employers felt no responsibility to pay their men a living wage. The labourers were demoralised because there was no incentive to work hard or to stay in work at all. The inflated poor-rates were a grievous burden on agriculture, hindering investment and enterprise, and crushing the small tenant farmer or freeholder. And apart from the allowance system there were complaints that in many areas the administration of relief was extremely lax, through the incapacity or carelessness of part-time overseers who were moreover subject to all kinds of local pressure. Finally, where there were poorhouses they were not seldom the scene of the utmost squalor and depravity through the mingling of all types of paupers, including the aged, the sick, the criminal, the insane and the children. In Scotland there was a contrasting picture. There was no legal right to relief, as in England, and no compulsion on local authorities to levy a poor rate, but much more reliance on charitable collections and mutual help among the poor. In consequence the total cost of relief was only a fraction of that in England, and the poor lived harder and died sooner. In Ireland there was no official system of relief of any kind.

The evils of the old Poor Law in England and Wales had long been recognised, but no solution had appeared other than the outright abolition of poor relief, which few would contemplate. In 1832 the Whig government set up a Royal Commission to inquire into the system—the first of many in the nineteenth century to examine social problems. Its chairman was Blomfield, Bishop of London, and one of its most eminent members was Nassau Senior, formerly Professor of Political Economy at Oxford, while one of the Assistant Commissioners was Edwin Chadwick, who had been Bentham's secretary and was to figure in almost every major inquiry for some time to come. The Commission collected evidence from all over the country, and in 1833 produced its

Report, which was widely published. This not only contained striking witness to all the abuses alleged against the old system, but argued the case for total reform with incisiveness and power. The remedies it proposed were simple and drastic. The allowance system was to be abolished, and with it all out-relief for the able-bodied and their families, who would be fed and clothed only if they entered the workhouse and stayed there. This was 'the workhouse test' of indigence, simple and self-acting, and to make the test real, conditions in the workhouse were to be less favourable than those of an 'independent labourer of the lowest class'. Here was the most direct application of the Utilitarian theory of motive—if idleness was made more unpleasant than work, people would work.

The Report carried conviction not only because it delineated with so much apparent truth the evils of the old Poor Law, but because it stressed the benefits that would follow from the new proposals. When the burden of indiscriminate relief had been lifted the guardians of the poor would be far better able to succour the truly unfortunate—the old, the sick and the children. With the reduction of the poor-rate more capital would be attracted to the land, and there would be work for everybody. Best of all, the labourer would benefit, because his employer would have to pay him a living wage; instead of having to beg for relief, he would be independent and self-reliant and no longer a stranger to the virtues of industry and thrift.

The Poor Law Amendment Act (1834) adopted completely the findings of the Commission, and set up a new and permanent Poor Law Commission to put the suggested remedies into effect. Its original members were Frankland Lewis, a Welsh country gentleman who had held minor posts in Tory ministries, J. G. Shaw-Lefevre, an under-secretary in the Colonial Office, and G. Nicholls, a bank manager and reputedly a model overseer of the poor in Southwell. Chadwick, to his justifiable chagrin, was appointed not as a member but as Secretary to the Commission, an office in which he proved both indefatigable and unmanageable. The Commission was not answerable to a minister and therefore not subject to the control of Parliament. It was given the widest powers to draft regulations, issue instructions and supervise the whole system of relief. Inspectors were appointed throughout the country whose reports would keep the Commission constantly informed of the way in which their instructions were being carried out. All parishes were to be combined by the Commission into unions large enough to maintain a workhouse of the kind now prescribed. No discretion was left to the guardians, elected by the ratepayers in each union, who replaced the overseers of the poor, and the Justices of the Peace lost all their powers in respect of relief. Nothing could have been more repugnant to the British tradition of entrusting the administration of public affairs to local and unpaid persons.

Whatever criticisms were made of the new Poor Law in action, its basic principles as set forth in the Report were virtually unchallenged during the nineteenth century, and any proposal that seemed to contradict its logic started under a severe disadvantage. If, however, the accusations made in the Report against the old Poor Law could be shown to be inaccurate, its whole argument would of course be weakened. Those accusations have been questioned in an article by Dr. Mark Blaug in the *Journal of Economic History, Vol. XXIII* (June 1963), 'The Myth of the Old Poor Law and the Making of the New'. In the first place this critic devalues the evidence relied on by the Commissioners, pointing out that they compiled no satisfactory statistics, and did not in fact know how many people were receiving relief. Their horrifying examples of the demoralising effects of the allowance system were often drawn from anecdotes of the kind that respectable citizens would delight to recount. As to the total cost of relief, it is suggested that 9s 9d per head of the whole population in a year of exceptional distress was not an intolerable charge. The increase in cost which was found alarming around 1830 was due not to abuse of poor relief but to increasing distress. As to the hardship to the farmer, it was mitigated by the fact that when the price of bread and therefore the cost of relief were highest the farmer was getting the best price for his wheat, while the allowance system enabled the poor still to buy bread. This argument, however, is weakened by the fact that the allowances were gradually scaled down until in 1825 they were on average one-third below the Speenhamland level. Finally, while it is admitted that the allowance system caused an increase in the population, this is explained not by a rise in the birth-rate but by a fall in the death-rate due to improved nutrition—a contention which requires more substantial proof.

The Commissioners soon came under criticism from contemporaries. Both the harshness of their régime and their dictatorial powers invited it; they were required, however, to lay their major rulings before Parliament, and there were frequent debates in which the cruelties of the new order were revealed by Tories as well as Radicals, assisted outside Parliament by the Press, *The Times* in particular. To working-class people the new system proclaimed that poverty was a crime to be punished by confinement in workhouses that, being no different from prisons, they called 'Bastilles'. The comparison was justified. Once admitted to a workhouse the pauper who left it forfeited all claim to relief. Tasks set to the inmates were of the most unpleasant kind, such as stone-breaking and oakum-picking. The sexes were rigorously separated and families were broken up. On the Commissioners' instructions (reversed, however, in 1842) there must be silence at meals. While children, the aged, and the able-bodied were supposed to be strictly separated, this was not found possible in most workhouses, and the severity prescribed for the able-bodied naturally set the tone for the whole establishment. It was with good reason that working-class people dreaded the possibility—almost a certainty if they had no relatives to care for them—of ending their days in a workhouse.

Were there any mitigating factors? Dr. McCord considers, on the basis of evidence from Tyneside, that the Commissioners tried to minimise the hardship caused by the new regulations and that on the whole paupers were better treated than under the old law. And it is true that each union had a medical officer and that education was supposed to be provided for workhouse children in special district schools. In general, however, it must be concluded that where the claims of humanity were recognised it was because the intentions of the Commissioners were not properly carried out. It was impossible, unless guardians and workhouse masters were to devote themselves to the organisation of squalor, to make conditions worse than those of the lowest-paid wage-earner; workhouse standards of buildings and fittings, heating and clothing were often better. What is more important, the 'workhouse test' was never enforced at all over a large part of the country. While in the south, where the Commissioners went to work first, they were favoured by unusual prosperity in 1835 and 1836, so that resistance was slight and the poor-rates went down, in the north in the next two years a depression set in, and mass unemployment made it impossible to apply the 'workhouse test'. Outdoor relief was never banned in the manufacturing districts of Lancashire and the West Riding of Yorkshire; it was in fact the only way of dealing with waves of unemployment in industry. Moreover there was organised and violent resistance to the building of the hated 'Bastilles'. The new Poor Law was regarded in the north as a third betrayal of the working class, following the Reform Act and the failure of the short-time campaign, and Richard Oastler, who had led the latter, now directed its organisation against the new Poor Law, with the support of Fielden, the Todmorden manufacturer, and J. R. Stephens, a fiery orator who had been expelled from the Methodist ministry, and this time their efforts met with at least local success.

G. M. Young and W. D. Handcock, editors of Vol. XII (I) of *English Historical Documents*, published in 1956, admitted that the hopes of the Commissioners were not fully achieved, but praised them for setting a new standard of administration—which may be granted—and considered that in their main task they had 'almost unqualified success', i.e. 'in restoring the threatened spirit of independence and industry. The Commission preserved, if they did not create, the Victorian doctrine of work on which the most characteristic achievements of the age depended.' It may not be unfair to describe this as an armchair judgment which rests upon a number of unproven assumptions. In many respects the Commissioners obviously failed. The new regulations did not in general reduce the cost of relief, which continued to be heavy in the south until agriculture revived. By maintaining the principle of settlement, whereby a person could only claim relief in the parish where he was born, they actively discouraged migration from the overpopulated agricultural areas to the industrial regions of the north, where the demand for labour was met by thousands of Irish immigrants instead. And as the century proceeded, many types of unfortunate people had to be provided for by other legislative and administrative means more humane than the new Poor Law.

3 Factory children; education; the abolition of slavery

During its first year the reformed Parliament passed a Factories Regulation Act which, while of small moment compared with the reform of the Poor Law, also broke new ground. Earlier Acts had dealt only with the employment of children in cotton mills, and had failed because there was no effective way of enforcing them. For this reason the Act promoted in 1819 by Sir Robert Peel, mill-owner and father of the statesman, forbidding the employment of children under nine and limiting the hours of those under sixteen, had had little effect. More than one inquiry was held, revealing widespread evils—excessive hours and much night work in ill-ventilated buildings, a large proportion of female and child labour, low wages, severe penalties for unpunctuality and other faults, and sometimes brutal treatment. It was proved that these conditions spelt illness, deformity and early death for thousands of workpeople. The smaller and less prosperous the undertaking, the more likely were these abuses to be found, but legislation was resisted by nearly all industrialists on the grounds of laissez-faire doctrine and the pressure of foreign competition.

This resistance was overcome by a remarkable combination of Yorkshire Tory landowners, Radical and Evangelical champions of the oppressed, adult spinners in Lancashire concerned for security of employment, and the Whig government. The first of these forces was led by Richard Oastler, a Tory land agent and Evangelical who had been active in securing the suppression of slavery, and who realised that the sufferings of many workers in English factories were no less than those of negroes on sugar plantations. The Yorkshire gentry who supported him shared the ideal which governed the political thinking of the young Disraeli —the well-run estate of a benevolent landowner, the natural leader of his people. They hated the manufacturers, who usually showed no such paternalism, and most of whom were Whigs who had been successfully challenging the landowners' grip on Parliament and government. In the House of Commons, after the failure of two further Acts passed in 1825 and 1831 to produce any effect, the campaign was taken up successively by Michael Sadler and Lord Ashley (later Earl of Shaftesbury), both Tories and Evangelicals. Ashley took over a Bill drafted by Sadler which restricted hours of work for persons under eighteen to ten, with no night work. This proposal had its origin in the short-time committees of Lancashire, whose real object was to reduce the working day to ten hours for workers of all ages, thus, they claimed, spreading employment and prosperity and widening the market for the products of the factories. The House of Commons, however, would not accept this Bill, and decided, by a majority of one, first to set up a Royal Commission to take evidence from both supporters and opponents of new legislation and to produce an impartial report. This was the opportunity of the Benthamites, who were well represented on the Commission. As firm believers in laissez-faire they were opposed to any regulation of the employment of adult male workers, though they were willing to allow that women and children needed the protection of the state— which, they pointed out, was not secured by Ashley's Bill, since ten hours made too long a working day for children, especially if they were to receive some education, a need which the Bill ignored. Largely as a result of this criticism Ashley's Bill was then defeated, and Althorp, Leader of the House of Commons, sponsored a different Bill, based on the Commission's report and drafted by Chadwick, which became the Factories Act of 1833.

The Act limited the hours of work to eight for children up to thirteen, forbidding altogether the employment of those under nine, and it was to apply in all textile factories except those working on lace and (for some purposes) silk. But the main improvement achieved by this measure was that instead of relying on informers to reveal breaches of the Act, inspectors were employed to make regulations, tour factories, and prosecute offending employers. The Act also scored the first success for the principle of compulsory education, for the factory children were to have two hours' schooling every day, but as no public money was advanced for this, and as it could in some cases be paid for by deduction from the children's meagre wages, the reality usually fell far short of the Commissioners' hopes. Nor was the limitation of hours properly enforced, for although a doctor's certificate was required to verify each child's age, parents, employers, doctors and magistrates often conspired to evade the law, and only after the registration of births was introduced in 1836 was this loophole partially stopped. It was also quite impossible for the four inspectors who were appointed to supervise the large areas put under their charge; one of them soon killed himself with overwork in the attempt.

The employers had a strong temptation to evade the provisions of the Act because it was difficult to run a textile mill unless both adults and children were at work, and the shift system for children which was expected to solve this problem usually did not work in practice. Parents were motivated in the same direction, being anxious to add the children's wages to the family income. As it was taken for granted at that time that able-bodied men of the poorer classes worked all day long and the women and children whenever they could, the attempt to enforce the Act was a struggle against the tide, a struggle which, moreover, could easily take on the character of a campaign of middle-class busybodies against the working class. The inspectors soon learned to be tactful, regarding the educational provision as the most important part of the Act, and interpreting their own functions as being mainly to keep the worse employers up to the standard of the best, who showed a real concern for their child employees. The progress of enforcement was slow and difficult, but the first real step had been taken, and the annual reports of the inspectors prepared the ground for later, more effective legislation.

If the reform of municipal government, with the establishment of an orderly and uniform national system and an approach to democratic control, was a triumph for the Benthamites, their efforts in the field of education resulted in a complete defeat of these principles at the hands of religious forces which were to yield little ground to secular reformers until the Education Act of 1870 was passed. Previous to this most of the organised schooling for the children of the poor was provided by the British and Foreign School Society, founded in 1807, which was undenominational, and the National Society for Promoting the Education of the Poor in the Principles of the Established Church, founded in 1811, which was Anglican. The latter had much the larger funds and many more schools, and claimed in 1831 to be educating half a million children. The method of teaching in the schools of both societies, the invention of which was disputed between them, was the monitorial system, whereby the single schoolmaster taught lessons to some of the older children which they repeated to the younger. It was remarkably cheap, since one teacher sufficed for several hundred children, and dreadfully mechanical, for the work was limited almost necessarily to rote-learning; but it was better than nothing.

Pressure for a national system of education came from the 'philosophic Radicals', whose desire for enlightenment and equality could be satisfied in no other way, and who could point to the systems already in operation in France and Prussia. Bills to promote a similar system in Britain were brought forward in 1820 by Brougham and in 1823 by Roebuck, another ardent follower of Bentham. Roebuck's was a complete scheme of schooling from seven to fourteen, each school to be locally and democratically managed, but the whole to be controlled by a minister of education. His Bill was hotly attacked from every quarter—by Peel, Althorp and O'Connell, and gained none but Radical support. A small beginning was made by the Whigs, however, thanks probably to Brougham's advocacy in the Cabinet. The government decided on an annual grant of £20,000 to help the two religious societies to expand and maintain their schools. It was allocated in proportion to their efforts, which meant that the National Society got four-fifths of the amount. With this modest measure the Radicals had for the moment to be satisfied, except that they managed to insert some educational provision into the Acts dealing with the factory children and the Poor Law.

Roebuck did not relax his efforts, which helped to produce a succession of three select committees of the House of Commons from 1834 to 1838. The last particularly emphasised the lack of religious and moral training as a cause of crime, for while the wretched state of many children in the new towns shocked humanitarians, their irreligion shocked believers even more. A further proposal was therefore made in 1839 which was quite ambitious in conception. A committee of the Privy Council was to administer the government grants and exercise a general supervision; the grants to the two societies were to be equalised, which would enable the British and Foreign greatly to expand; and a central college was to be set up to train teachers for both, their religious instruction being of a neutral kind. This scheme was furiously attacked by the Anglicans, who believed not only that all education must be founded on religious training, but that this was valueless unless it was confessional, i.e. in conformity with the doctrine of a particular church. Theirs being the established Church, its tenets must be taught in the schools, and it should superintend the whole education of the nation. So strong was the support for this view in both Houses of Parliament that the government had to give way to it, and therefore the existing arrangement was little changed. A committee of the Privy Council was indeed formed to supervise the spending of the government grants, but these remained proportional to the private contributions received by the two societies, except that they were supplemented by a government subsidy of one-third of the capital cost of new school buildings. Furthermore, inspectors of schools were now appointed for the first time to see that money was being wisely spent, but they were to be approved by the bishops and were to report to them as well as to the new committee. The Nonconformists had to wage a long but finally successful fight to obtain an equal footing in these matters. Halévy's verdict suggests that the government could have taken a bolder stride towards a national system of education, for he speaks of 'the tortuous and timid methods characteristic of Lord Melbourne's administration', but this was not the only government of the century to show timidity in the face of ecclesiastical fury, which long delayed the establishment of a national system of education.

Whereas in the matter of education the Whig government gave inadequate support to the Dissenters, it brought to fruition in Parliament a campaign of most strenuous propaganda led by Dissenters and Evangelicals for the abolition of slavery in the British Empire. So successful were the abolitionists in stirring public feeling that slavery was a prominent issue in the general election of 1830, and it was linked with the demand for parliamentary reform because the West Indian interest held certain rotten boroughs which assured it a hearing in the House of Commons. Fowell Buxton, succeeding to Wilberforce, urged the cause of abolition in the Commons, Brougham lent strong support in the House of Lords, and Stanley as Colonial Secretary produced in 1833 a plan whereby slaves could purchase their freedom in twelve years. The abolitionists, however, demanded more generous terms, especially when the government offered £20 million in compensation to assuage the complaints of the slave owners. Finally, large majorities in both Houses agreed that after a period of carefully regulated 'apprenticeship', six years for plantation slaves and only four years for house slaves, all were to receive their freedom. The declining profits of the sugar trade may, as a West Indian historian has maintained, help to explain why abolition did not meet with a stiffer resistance, but even he recognises the anti-slavery campaign as 'one of the greatest propaganda movements of all time'.

4 The Churches The most contentious subjects in British politics in the period after the Reform Act were the position of the established Church in England and the disabilities of the Nonconformists who remained outside it, and the even more debatable privileges of the Church of Ireland. For the moment the Church of England seemed to lie open to attack, weakened as it was by the state's concession of rights to Nonconformists in 1828 and to Roman Catholics in 1829, and by the advance of the Whigs and their Dissenting allies through parliamentary and municipal reform. Moreover the Church had seemed during the agitation of 1830 to 1832 to incur more bitter hatred from the general public than either the Crown or the aristocracy. Cobbett might say, 'The working clergy of the Church of England are, perhaps, taking them as a body, as good men as any in the world', but as an institution the Church was 'politically unpopular, socially exclusive, administratively corrupt'. (Gash, *Reaction and Reconstruction in English Politics*.)

It was the Church of Ireland to which the Whigs first gave their attention, for its large landed endowment, its inflated body of clergy and its claim to tithe constituted one of the heaviest burdens on the Irish peasantry and certainly the most resented. In 1833 the Whigs brought forward a measure more bold in its affront to the Church and in its attack on property rights than anything previously proposed. Even after their Bill had been modified to secure its passage through the House of Lords, it abolished the church 'cess' (or rate) and replaced it by a tax on clerical stipends, thus dealing a double blow at the Church's revenue, suppressed ten sees and dispensed with numbers of parish clergy who had no Protestant parishioners, and enabled tenants of the bishops to demand leases in perpetuity, whereby they would avoid any subsequent increase in their rents. The Whigs wished to go further, and apply the surplus income of the Church to other purposes, but such a step would have been obstructed by the House of Lords, as was their later attempt to abolish tithe in Ireland. They had, however, established the principle that instead of enjoying an absolute right to its property the Church's claims must be measured against the purposes it fulfilled.

In England, while few Dissenters aimed directly at the disestablishment of the Church, the opportunity seemed to have come to press for the removal of a great many disabilities and grievances of a practical kind. Dissenters objected in the first place to financial levies for the benefit of the Church of England— the church rates payable by householders in every parish, and tithe, though both were a standing grievance with others besides Nonconformists. They complained too that marriage and funeral services could be conducted only by clergymen of the Church of England, who were also solely entrusted with the registration of births. The universities of Oxford and Cambridge were closed to Nonconformists, so that it was impossible for them to obtain degrees, and in many areas schooling could be had only at one of the Anglican schools of the National Society. Melbourne had been prepared to remove some at least of these grievances, and when he was dismissed by the King in 1834, the discontent of the Dissenters boiled over into widespread agitation.

When Peel briefly replaced him in office, however, his attention was given almost entirely to measures concerning the reform of the Church on the one hand, and alleviating the Dissenters' grievances on the other, with the result that when the Whigs returned to power they built on Peel's foundations a number of measures which can be regarded as virtually agreed between the two parties. Peel introduced a measure, on which a Whig statute of 1836 was based, for the commutation of tithe, i.e. the payment as an addition to rent of a fixed sum of money instead of the annual contribution, amounting in all to £4 million, of a certain fraction of crops and livestock. The Irish Tithes Act of 1838 was on similar lines, and failed to provide, as the English Radicals had demanded, for the appropriation to secular purposes of tithe income surplus to the needs of the Church—which in Ireland were small compared to those of the Roman Catholic population. Also in pursuance of a measure which Peel had drafted but delayed, charters were granted to University College, which Bentham and his friends had founded in London as an institution free from all religious restrictions, and also to the University of London, which was to have authority to grant degrees, again irrespective of religious allegiance. It was Peel likewise who first prepared a Dissenters' Marriage Bill, providing for civil marriage before a Justice of the Peace, but Melbourne's government produced a more comprehensive measure: an Act of 1836 established a civil register of births, marriages and deaths for the whole of England, and enabled marriages to be celebrated in places of worship other than Anglican churches provided that a registrar was present, and in exceptional cases to be performed by a registrar.

To set against these important gains there were two notable defeats—the failure to relieve the Irish peasantry of the burden of tithes to maintain the Protestant Church of Ireland, and the rejection by the House of Commons of the Church Rates Bill (1837), which would have transferred the cost of upkeep of the church fabric from parishioners (who might be of any faith or none) to church funds, a reverse inflicted as much by Whig gentry in the House of Commons as by the Tory Opposition led by Peel.

The measure that held most promise of future reform of the Church was entirely due to Peel's initiative, though the Whigs allowed his creation to survive. This was the Ecclesiastical Commission, established in 1835 specifically to look into Church revenues, but made permanent in 1836 and empowered to prepare further proposals for reform. In this way an opening was made for the progressive forces within the Church of England, and, beginning with an equalisation of the incomes of bishoprics, the Commission went on to deal with pluralism and to reform cathedral chapters. The criticism of Dissenters was thus to some extent disarmed; with the removal of some of their worst grievances their campaign was thrown into confusion, and their alliance with the Whigs for the time being dissolved. The Church of England, on the other hand, went forward with renewed confidence and strength, to which the Oxford movement was soon to contribute a spiritual revival both powerful and uncompromising.

Such were the major reforms of the ministries of Grey and Melbourne in the years from 1833 to 1841. There can be no question that they were mainly inspired by the Utilitarian philosophy, though this was operative in varying degrees—merging in a general humanitarianism to secure the abolition of slavery, but elbowing it aside to make the new Poor Law, gaining a signal success in constructing the new fabric of borough government, but defeated by religious prejudice in the attempt to erect a national system of education. In all this work new administrative machinery was needed, beginning with the clerks who served under Peel's Commissioners of Police and advancing rapidly to produce the inspectors of factories and schools whose powers so alarmed a country unaccustomed to such professional mentors. Historians debate whether this advance was due more to the Benthamite emphasis on scientific enquiry and administration or to 'administrative momentum'—the tendency of any professionally staffed organisation to enlarge its size and competence. Whichever it may have been, it was fundamentally the growing complexity of society brought about by the technological revolution that was responsible for increasing government activity and therefore for an ever-growing bureaucracy—in an age whose watchword was laissez-faire.

5 The decline of the Whigs Once the struggle for parliamentary reform had been concluded the course of the Whig governments was difficult and uncertain. They could never rely completely on their Radical and Irish allies, and differences appeared among their own following on many of the leading issues of the time. But most of all they were dogged by failure in the management of finance. Starting badly with Lord Althorp's budget of 1831, which was so severely criticised in the Commons that it had to be completely recast, the Whigs continued to flounder throughout their time in office. When, as in 1833, a trade boom produced an unexpected surplus, troubles were hardly lessened, because there was then a general expectation of tax reductions, and any satisfaction of this kind given to urban interests produced an outcry from the landowners for a similar concession—usually for the removal of the malt tax. Althorp did however achieve by 1833 a reduction of expenditure by £3 million, the abolition of the house tax, and the lowering of duties on some three hundred articles of import. In the later thirties his successors were less fortunate, having to deal with the consequences of a depression of trade and an increased expenditure on the armed forces necessitated by Palmerston's ambitious foreign policy. Further reductions of tax rates were made in the hope that yield would not be reduced; when the hope proved false the government was faced with a succession of deficits which could only be covered by borrowing. They had never braced themselves to propose the only real solution of their constant budgetary difficulties—a restoration of the income tax—nor had they resolved the major question of the corn laws, the abolition of which was becoming the object of a great campaign outside Parliament. Either step would have split the ministry and invited utter defeat for the party.

Without any such catastrophe the Whigs were nevertheless in dire trouble in 1834, trouble precipitated, as on so many other occasions, by a dispute over Irish affairs. Yielding to Radical as well as Irish pressure, Lord John Russell declared that the revenues of the Irish Church were excessive, and a Radical motion to reduce its endowments was debated in the House. Stanley, Graham and two other ministers resigned in protest, soon to be followed by Grey, long anxious to be rid of the cares of office and now upset by covert negotiations with O'Connell carried on by some of his colleagues without his knowledge. Grey was succeeded by Melbourne, who was immediately faced with the possibility of a split in the Cabinet over the property of the Irish Church, and when Althorp succeeded to his father's peerage and a new Leader of the House of Commons had to be found, the necessary reconstruction of the Cabinet made the situation acute. Melbourne explained to the King that Lord John Russell had the best claim to succeed Althorp, but expressed some doubt as to whether a ministry could be formed under his own leadership. The King, motivated by his distrust of the Liberal Whigs, especially of Lord John Russell, and by his concern for the Protestant Church of Ireland, dismissed the Prime Minister and sent for the Duke of Wellington. As soon as Peel could get back from Italy, where he was travelling, the Duke handed over to him, and Peel formed a ministry, which Stanley and Graham, however, refused to join. Parliament was dissolved, and in the subsequent election the Conservatives, as they must now be called, gained a hundred seats—but not quite enough for a majority in the Commons. The result was also disquieting to Melbourne because the Whigs had lost ground to the Radicals. The combination of Whigs, Radicals and Irish, however, was adequate to outvote Peel's supporters more than once, finally on his Irish Tithe Bill. He resigned, and Melbourne returned at the head of a Cabinet much like his previous one.

The episode of 'Peel's Hundred Days' had not, however, been unimportant. The action of William IV in dismissing a Prime Minister who had the support of a majority of the House of Commons, and dissolving Parliament long before its term had expired in an attempt to produce a majority for the rival leader, was never to be repeated. It therefore marked not a reversal but a confirmation of the decline in the power of the monarchy which had taken place over the last fifty years. The King had tried to rally the forces of resistance to change, either by persuading Melbourne into a coalition with the Tories, or by replacing him with them, and both had failed. In future the monarch must accept the policy of a ministry supported by the House of Commons. This was the more certain because it was not possible after the reform of Parliament, as it had been earlier, for the ministers in office to 'make a House', i.e. to fill the Commons by means of patronage with members who would support them; a change of ministry now entailed a general election, with the risk of defeat.

In the short run, however, William IV had helped the Tories. In Parliament they had gained in numbers and confidence and Peel was marked out as their leader. He had moreover taken the opportunity of the election to issue to his constituents a statement of policy—the Tamworth Manifesto—which was really addressed to the whole country. Here was a creed of Conservatism for the nineteenth century. The party led by Peel would defend the national institutions against attack, but it would not go back on the reform of Parliament, and it would in future accept such reforms as were seen to be necessary. This was a guide to the party when in opposition as well as in office, and Peel followed it himself when on several occasions in the 1830s he voted for Whig measures he considered in harmony with Conservative principles.*

The Whigs returned in 1835 with no really secure basis of power. The crisis had shown up their dependence on the Radicals

* See K. H. Randell, *Politics and the People 1835-1850* in this series

and Irish, and the difficulties into which such allies could lead them. Their legislation was increasingly weakened by uncertainty and compromise; it revealed no clear principles or objectives, and where these could be discerned they were not very different from those of the Conservatives. The reform of this later period which was perhaps the most imaginative and beneficial—the penny post—was due in the main to a private initiative. The Whigs' reforming impulse had died away, perhaps because, as John Stuart Mill suggested, their measures had in fact satisfied the wishes of the bulk of the new electorate—not of all, however, for the Dissenters were sorely disappointed, and the free traders frustrated by the government's failure to deal with the corn laws. Still less were the Radicals satisfied. Russell in 1837 declared the 'finality' of the reform of Parliament achieved in 1832, and the only advance on that position was the Cabinet's resolve to treat the ballot as an 'open question'. The depression that descended on the country in 1836, accompanied as it was by bad harvests, budget deficits and increased taxes, sapped the spirit of the country and the confidence of the government.

What cheer the Whigs could find in these circumstances came from an unexpected quarter. When Victoria succeeded her uncle on the throne in 1837 she soon came to place quite remarkable trust in Lord Melbourne and gave her favour unmistakably to the Whigs, an advantage they did not fail to exploit to hold their supporters in the general election that followed her accession. In 1839, however, the ministry's majority in the House of Commons shrank to a handful through the desertion of some of the Radicals, and Melbourne resigned. The Queen sent for Peel, who, much in need of a sign of royal confidence in view of the doubtful position in the Commons, asked her to appoint Tory Ladies of the Bedchamber in place of the Whig ladies, mostly relatives of politicians, who had so far been her companions. She refused, Peel declined office, and Melbourne returned. The affair increased her popularity with the people, and that of the Whigs, but she had in fact been wrong to refuse Peel's request; put with more tact and grace it might, however, have been granted. The Whigs then continued in office, though hardly in power, till 1841, when their rule came to an end through a miscalculation. A general election would not be due until 1843 or 1844, but the government would be much strengthened if it could gain a sound majority in the House of Commons. The Queen was more anxious than Melbourne to try this expedient, and so dissolved Parliament. If the Whigs had declared for the free import of corn they would have made gains in the boroughs to compensate for their losses in the counties. In fact they had no better proposal than a fixed corn duty, and they lost in both. There is little doubt that a great many Radicals voted Conservative, as O'Connor, the Chartist leader, urged them to do, expecting to gain more from an independent posture than from being tied to the Whigs. The election gave the Conservatives a clear lead over all their opponents, and the era of Whig rule was at an end.

The Whigs, despite the dismal record of their later years, had much to their credit. In many ways it is true that their outlook was limited by the influence of birth and tradition. The punishment of the 'Swing' rioters, and later of the labourers of Dorset who had done no more than try to obtain a living wage by combining together—though illegally sealing their union with an oath—shows that the Whigs differed little from the Tories in their fear of the lower classes and their readiness to repress them. Their rule had not been without its failures—in Ireland, where failure was no uncommon story, and in management of the country's finances, where there was less excuse. On the other hand, these aristocrats had in two respects transcended the limitations natural to their class. They had seen the need to make a place in the constitution for the rising middle class, and they had deliberately set out on a course of systematic reform. They had thereby averted a threatened revolution, and directed the country towards a process of peaceful adjustment which was proof against the stresses of change more rapid than it had ever before known.

Chronological Table

1815 Treaties of Vienna   Corn Law
1816 Repeal of Income Tax   Agrarian riots   Spa Fields riot
1817 Suspension of Habeas Corpus
   March of the Blanketeers   Pentrich Rising
1818 General election
1819 Peterloo   The Six Acts
1820 Accession of George IV; general election   The Queen's trial
   Cato Street plot   Bonnymuir riot
1822 Peel Home Secretary   Death of Castlereagh; Canning Foreign
   Secretary
1823 Act to permit reciprocal trade treaties
   Foundation of the Catholic Association in Ireland
1824 Repeal of the Combination Acts
1825 New Combination Act   Financial crisis
1826 General election   Trade slump
1827 Canning Prime Minister (February)
   Death of Canning (August); Goderich Prime Minister
1828 Wellington Prime Minister (January)
   Corn Law   Repeal of Test and Corporation Acts
1829 Catholic Emancipation passed by Parliament
   Establishment of Metropolitan Police
1830 'Swing' riots   Accession of William IV;
   General election   Grey Prime Minister
1831 First Reform Bill; general election; second and third
   Reform Bills
1832 Resignation and return of Grey's ministry; Reform Act passed
   General election
1833 Trial of the Tolpuddle labourers   Factories Regulation Act
   First grant for education   Abolition of slavery
1834 Poor Law Amendment Act
   Resignation of Grey (July); Melbourne Prime Minister
   Peel Prime Minister (November)
1835 General election (January); resignation of Peel (April);
   Melbourne Prime Minster   Municipal Corporations Act
1836 Commutation of tithe; Ecclesiastical Commission established
1837 Accession of Victoria; general election
   Act for registration of births, marriages and deaths
1839 Bedchamber crisis
1841 General election; resignation of Melbourne; Peel Prime Minister

Further Reading

Of the general works which include the period, E. Halévy, *A History of the English People in the Nineteenth Century* (Ernest Benn, 1960) is a full narrative, balanced and often enlightening. E. L. Woodward, *The Age of Reform, 1815-1870* in the Oxford History of England (Oxford University Press, 2nd edition 1962) is reliable. A. Briggs, *The Age of Improvement, 1783-1867* (Longmans, 1959) is a stimulating outline.

R. J. White, *Waterloo to Peterloo* (Penguin, 1968) is a very readable account. D. Read, *Peterloo* (Manchester University Press, 1958) is a careful examination not only of the event but of its background and aftermath.

G. B. A. M. Finlayson, *England in the eighteen-thirties: decade of reform* (Edward Arnold, 1969) gives a useful account of the reform measures.

H. Perkin, *The Origins of Modern English Society, 1780-1880* (Routledge and Kegan Paul, 1969) is an ambitious attempt to unravel the interactions of social forces; stimulating, but must be read with caution. E. P. Thompson, *The Making of the English Working Class* (Gollancz, 1963) draws on a great fund of information and throws new light in many places, but conclusions conform to Marxist doctrine. The same comments apply to a study of a single episode in the period, *Captain Swing*, by E. J. Hobsbawm and G. Rudé (Lawrence and Wishart, 1969). J. L. and B. Hammond, *The Skilled Labourer, 1760-1832* (Longmans, 1920) deals with the various types of artisans and their discontents, making full use of Home Office papers. Samuel Bamford, *Days in the Life of a Radical* (McGibbon and Kee, 1967) is a valuable description of the movement by a member of the working class as literate as he was active. *The Autobiography of William Cobbett*, ed. W. Reitzel (Faber and Faber, 1967) is fascinating.

Political and constitutional developments are dealt with in a number of recent studies, but J. R. M. Butler, *The Passing of the Great Reform Bill* (Longmans, 1914) is still a reliable narrative.

A. Mitchell, *The Whigs in Opposition, 1815-1830* (Oxford University Press, 1967) is an analysis of party politics and a closely documented study of the behaviour of various groups in the House of Commons. A. S. Foord, *His Majesty's Opposition* (Oxford University Press, 1964) discusses the way the parties saw themselves and the growing recognition of the role of the Opposition. G. I. T. Machin, *The Catholic Question in English Politics, 1820-1830* (Oxford University Press, 1964) provides a detailed narrative and an assessment of attitudes and policies. N. Gash, *Mr. Secretary Peel* (Longmans, 1961) is a thorough examination of Peel's work first in Ireland and then at the Home Office. The same author's *Politics in the Age of Peel* (Longmans, 1953) is a most valuable enquiry into the working of the representative system after the first Reform Act, and his *Reaction and Reconstruction in English Politics* (Oxford University Press, 1965), a set of essays, gives fresh insights into political themes of the 1830s. G. Kitson Clark, *Peel and the Conservative Party* (F. Cass, 1964) examines Peel's tactics and his relations with his colleagues. Benjamin Disraeli's *Coningsby* (Dent, 1959), provides a highly individual view of Tory politics under a thin fictional disguise.

The following biographies may be recommended:

A. Aspinall, *Brougham and the Whig Party* (University of Manchester, 1927)

J. V. P. Rolo, *George Canning* (Macmillan, 1965)

C. J. Bartlett, *Castlereagh* (Macmillan, 1966)

W. R. Brock, *Lord Liverpool and Liberal Toryism* (F. Cass, 1967)

D. Cecil, *The Young Melbourne; Lord M.* (Constable, 1954)

G. Wallas, *The Life of Francis Place, 1771-1854* (Allen and Unwin, 1925)

W. D. Jones, *Prosperity Robinson* (Macmillan, 1967)

J. L. and B. Hammond, *Lord Shaftesbury* (F. Cass, 1969)

S. E. Finer, *The Life and Times of Edwin Chadwick* (Methuen, 1952)

Index